WALKING
with
JESUS

WALKING
with
JESUS

Devotions for
Advent & Christmas

Editors of *Mornings with Jesus*

A GUIDEPOSTS DEVOTIONAL

Walking with Jesus

Published by Guideposts
100 Reserve Road, Suite E200
Danbury, CT 06810
Guideposts.org

Acknowledgments

Every attempt has been made to credit the sources of copyrighted material used in this book. If any such acknowledgment has been inadvertently omitted or miscredited, receipt of such information would be appreciated.

Scripture quotations marked (CEB) are taken from the *Common English Bible*. Copyright © 2011 by Common English Bible.

Scripture quotations marked (ESV) are taken from *The Holy Bible, English Standard Version*. Copyright © 2001 by Crossway Bibles, a division of Good News Publishers. Used by permission. All rights reserved.

Scripture quotations marked (GW) are taken from *GOD'S WORD®*. Copyright © 1995, 2003, 2013, 2014, 2019, 2020 by God's Word to the Nations Mission Society. Used by permission.

Scripture quotations marked (KJV) are taken from the *King James Version of the Bible*.

Scripture quotations marked (MSG) are taken from *The Message*. Copyright © 1993, 2002, 2018 by Eugene H. Peterson.

Scripture quotations marked (NASB) are taken from the *New American Standard Bible®*, Copyright © 1960, 1971, 1977, 1995, 2020 by The Lockman Foundation. All rights reserved.

Scripture quotations marked (NIV) are taken from *The Holy Bible, New International Version®, NIV®*. Copyright © 1973, 1978, 1984, 2011 by Biblica, Inc. Used by permission. All rights reserved worldwide.

Scripture quotations marked (NKJV) are taken from the *New King James Version®*. Copyright © 1982 by Thomas Nelson. Used by permission. All rights reserved.

Scripture quotations marked (NLT) are taken from the *Holy Bible, New Living Translation*. Copyright © 1996, 2004, 2007, 2015 by Tyndale House Foundation. Used by permission of Tyndale House Publishers Inc., Carol Stream, Illinois. All rights reserved.

Scripture quotations marked (NRSV) are taken from the *New Revised Standard Version Bible*. Copyright © 1989 by the Division of Christian Education of the National Council of the Churches of Christ in the United States of America. Used by permission. All rights reserved.

Cover design by Pamela Walker, W Design Studio
Interior design by Mullerhaus
Cover photo by Dreamstime
Typeset by Aptara, Inc.

Special thanks to Amanda Ericson, Kaylin Kaupish, and Valentina Chiofalo.

ISBN 978-1-961126-51-0 (softcover)
ISBN 978-1-961126-52-7 (epub)

Printed and bound in the United States of America

While shepherds watched their flocks by night,
all seated on the ground,
an angel of the Lord came down,
and glory shone around.
"Fear not," said he for mighty dread
had seized their troubled mind
"glad tidings of great joy I bring
to you and all mankind."

Nahum Tate

An Advent Prayer
by Bob Hostetler

GOD OF HOPE, thank You for giving us new birth into a living hope through the resurrection of Jesus Christ. Thank you for giving us an inheritance that can never perish, spoil, or fade.

Our hope does not put us to shame, because Your love has been poured out into our hearts. Remind us that the Scriptures were written to teach us and that the encouragement they provide gives us hope. Grant that we may overflow with hope by the power of the Holy Spirit.

GOD OF PEACE, at the first Christmas Your angel announced, "Glory to God in the highest heaven, and on earth peace to those on whom His favor rests." (Luke 2:14, NIV) Thank You for the peace Jesus promised, not as the world gives, but willing, deep, and abiding peace.

Grant that we may live at peace with everyone, making every effort to do what leads to peace. Let the peace of Christ rule in our hearts, now and forever.

GOD OF JOY, let all who take refuge in You be glad; let them ever sing for joy. Grant that as Jesus promised, His joy may be in us and our joy may be complete.

Help us learn that, though we may grieve, our grief will turn to joy. Teach us to always pray with joy. Grant us such love and faith that we may always be filled with an inexpressible and glorious joy.

GOD OF LOVE, You demonstrated Your love for us in this: While we were still sinners, Christ died for us. I trust in Your unfailing love. Teach me to love You with all my heart, soul, mind, and strength.

Teach me to love my neighbor, to love my enemies, and to do good to all. Help me to remain in Your love. Help me to do everything in love, as I live by faith in the Son of God, who loved me and gave Himself for me.

AMEN

INTRODUCTION

Christmas is approaching—rejoice!

We look forward to its festivities, togetherness, and comforting traditions. Still, as the days get shorter and our to-do lists grow ever longer, we may find ourselves losing focus on what Christmas and the season are about: the birth of the Messiah and how He will come again. *Walking with Jesus: Devotions for Advent and Christmas* is a loving reminder of how Advent, the journey to Christmas, began and how it can continue to draw us closer to Christ. The daily devotions in this book are a gentle nudge away from the distractions of the world and back to Jesus.

Advent, which means "coming" or "arrival" in Latin, isn't mentioned in the Bible. Instead, the tradition grew among Christians in Europe more than a millennium ago, as a time when the faithful prepared for Christmas's annual arrival and the second coming of Christ. However, we can find glimmers of it in Bible passages. Advent is a time for us to reflect on the first Christmas and how Christ manifests in our everyday lives, as well as a time to prepare ourselves for His next days on earth.

Beyond wreaths and calendars, Advent has a profound spiritual dimension, and *Walking with Jesus* allows us to refresh and redirect our faith. We have the opportunity to reconnect with our spiritual foundation, to the quiet inward space where the soul resides. Reading this devotional and honoring the holy weeks of Advent can offer us comfort, tranquility, and spiritual nourishment.

Daily devotionals have become increasingly popular for a reason: Reading them is a manifestation of our desire to know God and understand His expectations of us, a longing that predates the hermit saints of early Christianity, as the Old Testament shows us.

> For the Lord gives wisdom;
> from his mouth come knowledge and understanding.
> Proverbs 2:6 (NIV)

You may already be familiar with the beloved publication *Mornings With Jesus*. The devotions in *Mornings with Jesus* have so inspired readers that we have collected a select few of them here for you. The writers, women of faith from all walks of life, share their unique takes on each Advent week's theme, inviting you to contemplate and steady the course of your own faith life.

This year, Advent begins on Sunday, December 3. Every week, anchored by a Sunday leading up to Christmas, has a theme that helps inform our understanding of Christ and our journey with Him:

HOPE is a balm for our worries and anxieties. As we enter the first week of Advent, we are invited to set aside our troubles and breathe freely, secure in the faith that we are Jesus', just as He is ours. Hope gives us strength and resilience, given by God with love to lighten our loads.

> May the God of hope fill you with all joy and peace as
> you trust in him, so that you may overflow with hope
> by the power of the Holy Spirit.
> Romans 15:13 (NIV)

PEACE permeates Advent's second week, offering clarity, perspective, and calm. We may be tested by events and experiences, but God's loving presence is a constant, reassuring touch. Entreat Him to bestow it in ever-wider circles: to ourselves, our loved ones, our communities, and the world we all share.

> Peace I leave with you; my peace I give you. I do not
> give to you as the world gives. Do not let your hearts
> be troubled and do not be afraid.
> John 14:27 (NIV)

JOY comes with the certainty that Christ was born among us to save us and will return to us one day. With Christmas drawing near, we are buoyant as we approach the moment God gave His greatest gift to us, Jesus the Redeemer.

> ...The angel said to them, "Do not be afraid.
> I bring you good news that will cause great joy for all the people."
> Luke 2:10 (NIV)

Love, the theme of Advent's final Sunday, defines our relationship with the living God. The Bible gives us countless examples of God's steadfast devotion—and even today who hasn't seen God's grace upon their own life? He loves us in His perfect way despite all our innumerable imperfections.

> Love is patient, love is kind. It does not envy,
> it does not boast, it is not proud....
> It always protects, always trusts, always hopes, always perseveres.
> 1 Corinthians 13: 4, 7 (NIV)

Walking with Jesus offers three daily devotions—personal stories with spiritual resonance—that mirror and examine the week's theme and carry through God's lessons in a modern world. You might find it best to read the three devotions at different points of your day: perhaps as you wake, another at midday, and a third before bed. Or you might choose to read them together to immerse yourself in the message and let it permeate your spirit. Each devotion also contains a faith step—a question or suggestion to help you refine your spiritual path. Consider reading the devotional with family members and friends to discuss your interpretations. Even if you do not have a daily devotion reading habit, Advent is a powerful time to incorporate devotions into your worship practice.

At the end of this book, you'll find a dedicated space for your reflections and memories. You can use these pages to jot down notes and insights about the devotions, note your progress with one of the faith steps given, write favorite scriptures, or doodle a holiday object that makes you smile. You can even use the pages as a time capsule to record what made this year's Advent and Christmas special to you and your family. Imagine the joy you and your loved ones will have looking back at these moments captured in time!

As we embark on a new Advent and Christmas and the holy celebration at its heart, we wish you all the hope, peace, joy, and love of the season!

Lisa Guernsey

HOPE

Show me your ways, LORD,
teach me your paths.
Guide me in your truth and teach me,
for you are God my Savior,
and my hope is in you all day long.

Psalm 25: 4–5 (NIV)

FIRST SUNDAY OF ADVENT, DECEMBER 3

The people who walked in darkness have seen a great light; those who dwelt in a land of deep darkness, on them has light shone. Isaiah 9:2 (ESV)

I LOVE THE SYMBOLS WE use during Advent and Christmas. Each year, our family sets up an Advent wreath. The circle shape represents the gift of eternity that is given to us because of Jesus. The evergreen boughs remind us that the love of Jesus is constant, endures, and is for all seasons. And each candle represents a specific part of the blessing of the Incarnation.

When we light the first candle, on the first Sunday in Advent, we call it the prophecy or "hope" candle. Everything recorded in the Old Testament prophesied the coming of Emmanuel, who would bring light into our darkness.

The flickering glow of that first candle stirs our hope. The Light has come, dwells with us, and will come again.

Advent is an interesting time of waiting for something that we already know has happened: Jesus's birth. We also look ahead to His return. As we find the prophecies that pointed to His birth, we also find Scripture that hints at the end of the story. Just as Israel eagerly waited for their Messiah, we eagerly wait for Christ's return at the end of time. While we wait, we are comforted by the light He brings into our daily lives. His presence with us casts aside the shadows of sin, fear, and doubt. His example kindles the flame of faith in our hearts. His grace warms and changes our hearts so that we can offer love to others in His name. —SHARON HINCK

FAITH STEP: *Create an Advent wreath—a drawing on a paper placemat, or a ring of small candles in holders, or a traditional one from a store—embellished with pine boughs. Light (or color in) the first candle and thank Jesus for being the promised Light.*

FIRST SUNDAY IN ADVENT, DECEMBER 3

And his name will be the hope of all the world. Matthew 12:21 (NLT)

HAVE YOU NOTICED ABOUT THIS time of year how often we hear the word "hope"? Perhaps that's not by accident.

We will always hear of hurts and disappointments, and even experience them ourselves throughout the year. But at Christmastime needs rise to the surface like the fat of rich cream. I see that in the newspaper headlines, Internet news features, and in the heart-tugging requests of people who often comment on my blogs about the discouragement in their lives. Everyone wants—and needs—hope.

Perhaps the cheerful celebrations at Christmas stir up an intense longing and desire for encouragement. Those "without" look into the windows of those "with" and can often feel the weight of despair and loneliness exaggerated.

Cries for help do reach willing servants, moved by love and compassion to meet the most desperate needs. Churches and other helpful organizations search for impoverished families to "adopt," while nonprofit groups beg for more to supply the greatest demands. But we cannot meet them all. And at best, even the most generous philanthropists can't restore the losses and fill the stockings of every person in crisis.

There is, however, One Who can. He may choose not to fix every physical need until heaven. But the soul's most pressing need, "the hopes and fears of all the years," has already been met. Jesus, God's most precious gift, is the hope of all the world.

Our pocketbooks will empty, but our hearts can remain full year-round. When others long for hope and encouragement, don't forget to also share with them the gift that lasts forever: the good news of Jesus. —REBECCA BARLOW JORDAN

FAITH STEP: *This Advent, do without something you enjoy, and give the "savings" to someone in need. As you do, share with them the hope.*

First Sunday of Advent, December 3

We have this as a sure and steadfast anchor of the soul, a hope that enters into the inner place behind the curtain, where Jesus has gone as a forerunner on our behalf. . . . Hebrews 6:19–20 (ESV)

A HUSH FELL AS THE lights dimmed to near darkness and the speaker described the condition of the world the Baby Jesus would be born into.

God's people had long been oppressed by the Roman government. Those were dark days back then, full of hopelessness for the Israelites. The somber mood in the worship center deepened the sense of hopelessness. It seemed we could feel a fraction of what the Israelites had felt.

And then into the darkness a small flame erupted. The flicker of light came from the Advent wreath at the front of the church, a tiny glow that shattered the darkness. Darkness cannot exist where light is, and when darkness is extinguished, hope is born.

How fitting that hope is the theme for the first of the four weeks of Advent. Hope comes first, hope for the peace and joy and love we cannot find on our own and never in real and lasting measure apart from Christ.

Each year as December rolls along, my spirit simply wants to be quiet and digest Advent's themes, the realities of each of the weeks, instead of hurrying through the chaos. I long to reflect and finish the year with the messages of Advent on my heart.

Advent is for filling up on hope; what a refreshing thought!

As today's verse says, Jesus is the forerunner of our lives. And with Him in the lead, we can welcome the days ahead full of hope. —ERIN KEELEY MARSHALL

FAITH STEP: *Remind yourself of H.O.P.E. with these responses to Jesus for being our great hope: Hallelujah Overflowing in Praises Eternal.*

MONDAY, DECEMBER 4

But those who hope in the Lord will renew their strength. They will soar with wings like eagles: They will run and not grow weary, they will walk and not be faint. Isaiah 40:31 (NIV)

DO YOU REMEMBER WHEN YOU were a child how unbearable the long wait before Christmas was? Being wild with anticipation for the boundless goodies and toys were just days away? Going to sleep on Christmas Eve was near impossible. I could hardly wait!

I am still not great at waiting. There has been a lot of waiting in my life. Waiting to get married. Waiting for my babies to be born. Waiting to be published. Then there are all the mundane hours of waiting. Like waiting for laundry to get done or for kids to finish going to the bathroom. You will not believe how much time I have spent knocking on bathroom doors asking, "Are you done in there, for goodness sake?" So much waiting.

In Isaiah 40:31 (NIV), it says, "Those who hope in the Lord will renew their strength..." In the King James translation, it says, "They that wait upon the Lord shall renew their strength..." Hope and waiting seem like opposites. Hope seems so positive and uplifting and waiting seems horrible and angst ridden.

But hope and waiting go hand in hand. We can wait because we have hope. We wait on Jesus' timing because our hope is in Him. It is the very essence of Christmas. All that waiting for the Messiah. All that hoping. And then there it was. God with us. I will never like waiting. Yet I am filled with hope for all that tomorrow holds. Prayers answered, friendships relished and miracles arriving. Like the One that arrived so long ago. A babe wrapped in swaddling clothes. He was worth the wait. —SUSANNA FOTH AUGHTMON

FAITH STEP: *Write down three things that you are waiting for right now and remind yourself that there is hope in the waiting.*

MONDAY, DECEMBER 4

So we fix our eyes not on what is seen, but on what is unseen, since what is seen is temporary, but what is unseen is eternal. 2 Corinthians 4:18 *(NIV)*

WHEN OUR CHILDREN WERE YOUNG, we wanted them to be engaged in our family Advent devotions. Besides the symbolic candles in the Advent wreath, we created a basket full of small boxes. After Bible reading time, one of the children would choose a box and open it, and create a "devotional thought" based on the object inside. A marble, a thimble, a wooden butterfly, or a seashell. Whatever they found, they would explain some truth about Jesus: a marble in our hand, the way our Creator holds the world. A thimble protects our thumb, as Jesus protects our souls. A butterfly dies and is reborn, as we will be one day because of the death and Resurrection of Jesus.

Each tangible object—a thing that is seen—could remind us of a larger truth—the thing that is not seen.

Some days it's a challenge to see Jesus at work in our lives. The temporary "what is seen" fills our entire field of vision, distracting us and even causing us to obsess over it. Our days fill with goals we want to reach, people we wish would change, troubles that grab our focus. Yet in the midst of our day, those tangible objects and visible events can springboard our thoughts toward the eternal.

The goals that feel overwhelming can remind us of our reliance on Christ and His provision. The irritating family member can provide a place to practice Jesus's call to forgiveness. Our struggle with pain can call to mind the beautiful mercy of Jesus and the promise of new, whole bodies one day.

Each day becomes an adventure when we find ways to look beyond what is seen, to what is eternal. —SHARON HINCK

FAITH STEP: *Look around the place where you're sitting. Choose one tangible object and think of a way it can remind you of a truth about Jesus.*

MONDAY, DECEMBER 4

"Behold, you will conceive in your womb and bring forth a Son, and shall call His name JESUS. He will be great, and will be called the Son of the Highest; and the Lord God will give Him the throne of His father David. And He will reign over the house of Jacob forever, and of His kingdom there will be no end." Luke 1:31–33 (NKJV)

WHEN I WAS A TEENAGER I read *Two from Galilee* by Marjorie Holmes. It made a huge impression on me because of how Mary was portrayed. Instead of the larger-than-life character she becomes in so many of our nativity narratives, Holmes imagined her as just a girl. She was special, yes. But mostly she was a normal teenager, like I was at the time.

Mary must have felt overwhelmed by the charge the angel gave her. Even though it was the honor of the ages, it was also the ultimate responsibility. How did she know she could do it? Further, what would make the hardships of her situation worth it?

I believe Mary grasped a concept that eludes many during the Christmas season, represented by the first candle of Advent: hope. As a Hebrew child she would have been taught to look for the Messiah, to place her hope in the promise of His coming. The angel offered the fulfillment of that promise, and a chance for Mary to participate in it.

When the hardships of your situation seem impossible, how do you know you can do it? Our hope is the same as Mary's. Jesus the Messiah, Hope of the entire world. When we allow Him to be born in us, we participate in the first miracle of Christmas. The miracle of hope. —GWEN FORD FAULKENBERRY

FAITH STEP: *Is your hope in the Messiah today? Make a list of situations you see that look hopeless. Pray for Jesus to breathe hope into them, and to show you how you might participate.*

TUESDAY, DECEMBER 5

We also have the prophetic message as something completely reliable, and you will do well to pay attention to it, as to a light shining in a dark place, until the day dawns and the morning star rises in your hearts. 2 Peter 1:19 (NIV)

EVERY DECEMBER I START REMINDING my husband that there are only three weeks left until the days start to get longer again. And every time I do, he jokes that he knew there was a reason he married me! Steve isn't fond of darkness descending early, so he loves to hear that, when daylight diminishes to its briefest, it's on the brink of getting longer again.

The saying "It is always darkest just before dawn" usually refers to the twenty-four-hour day-and-night cycle, but it also applies to the seasonal changes of the sun's setting and rising. That saying can also apply to the dark times we face in life. When we're in the middle of a painful season and we feel our hope falter, we can trust that Jesus—the Light of the world—will arrive to help us just in time.

It is significant that the Bible tells of the kings who followed a star through the darkness to find the young Savior. He came to be with us amid the darkness of Israel's captivity, and He shined His light everywhere He went as He drew people to salvation. More than once Jesus called Himself the light of the world (John 9:5), but during the Sermon on the Mount, He also told His disciples, "You are the light of the world. A town built on a hill cannot be hidden" (Matthew 5:14, NIV).

Can you picture it, the Light of the world up there on the mountain, inviting His own to identify with Him, to join the kingdom that shines and cannot be hidden? It's a majestic image, a holy one that we're part of as believers in Him. Where does His light shine out from you in this world? —ERIN KEELEY MARSHALL

FAITH STEP: *Ask Jesus to help you live full of His light among the world where He placed you. Thank Him for inviting you to be part of His light.*

TUESDAY, DECEMBER 5

In his great mercy he has given us new birth into a living hope through the resurrection of Jesus Christ from the dead. 1 Peter 1:3 (NIV)

"WHAT IS IT ABOUT THIS family and hope?" my youngest grandson asked. "We have a cousin named Hope, and there's hope everywhere in this house!"

I love his exuberance on the subject. Ours *is* a house filled with hope. It shows up in books on the bookshelves, mugs, pictures... it's everywhere. I may have mentioned before that a young visitor came to our home and counted the items in our house bearing the word *hope*. She stopped counting at forty-seven.

It is a house filled with Jesus, our Living Hope.

When the FedEx delivery guy steps into the family room with a box, I pray he says, "What is it about this family and hope?" When our hope-filled friends bring their hope-deprived friends with them for a group outing or a meal, may that question be on their minds too. When neighbors bring a jar of honey from their beehives or a small neighborly remembrance at Christmas, may they also leave saying, "What is it about this family and hope?"

What is it? We have devoted ourselves to our Living Hope—Jesus. He infuses every moment with a new, eternal perspective. In troubled times, we cling to Him. In victorious times, we thank Him for the gift. He is the source of our hope. Though some may consider our house a hope museum, because of the presence of Jesus, it is instead a *living* tribute. —CYNTHIA RUCHTI

FAITH STEP: *What in your home communicates a message of hope? Your welcome mat? The Bible on your coffee table? How will you enhance the hope theme?*

TUESDAY, DECEMBER 5

Wait for the Lord; Be strong and let your heart take courage;
Yes, wait for the Lord. Psalm 27:14 (NASB)

THE LAST YEAR HAS BEEN a year of waiting. John and I have been waiting to adopt from the foster care system again. We've waited for home studies. We've waited for paperwork. We've waited to be matched with a child. We are still waiting, and it breaks my heart to think there is a child waiting and wondering if he or she will ever have a forever home. Not having a family is hard for a child. Waiting to open our home is hard too. It's not like waiting for an event or a special gift. We're waiting to share good news: "We want you to be ours" and "Come and see your new home."

You'd think the waiting would be discouraging. Instead it's given us fearless trust. Some of the themes from Psalm 27 have echoed in my heart this year: "Be gracious to me and answer me" (Psalm 27:7). "Your face, O Lord, I shall seek" (Psalm 27:8), and "I would have despaired unless I had believed that I would see the goodness of the Lord in the land of the living" (Psalm 27:13).

Fearless trust only comes when our prayers aren't answered right away. It's then we must remember Who Jesus is and what He has done for us. In the case of foster children who need forever homes, it's remembering that Jesus loves them even more than we do, and He's already picked the perfect child for our home.

Waiting is hard. Waiting on the Lord takes strength and courage. But someday the wait will be over, and at the end of the wait we'll receive Jesus's perfect answer... whatever that answer may be. *Whoever* that answer may be. —TRICIA GOYER

FAITH STEP: *Create a "waiting" journal. Record the things you're waiting for, and then record Jesus's answers. Keeping track of the many ways that Jesus answers your prayers will give you the strength and the courage!*

WEDNESDAY, DECEMBER 6

Now faith is confidence in what we hope for and assurance about what we do not see. This is what the ancients were commended for. Hebrews 11:1–2 (NIV)

FOR AS LONG AS I can remember, I have harbored huge dreams. With the passage of time, they change. As a young woman, I dreamed of finding a funny, handsome man to love who would love me back. After I was married to my funny, handsome husband, Scott, I dreamed of following my passion of storytelling. This was coupled with my dream of raising a family of beautiful boys with hearts for Jesus. Today, Scott and I realized another dream. We picked up the keys to our first home: a dream we had thought would never come true. It was too big, too grandiose, too unreal to hope for, yet . . . here we are. In a miraculous turn of events, with the hand of Jesus, the help of parents, and the prayers of friends, we are seeing the impossible become possible.

This is the currency that Jesus deals in. Prayers. Dreams. Promises. Possibilities. He is a Savior without limits. He out-blesses us, out-gives us, and out-loves us at every turn. He knows a little something about hopes and dreams. For thousands of years, the Israelites waited in hope, believing in the face of unfathomable odds that the heavenly Father would keep His promise and send a Savior: His one and only Son. We can dream, standing in that same hope and rock-solid place of faith, knowing that Jesus, the hope of heaven, has come and will come again. That is more than a dream come true.

In this Advent season, revel in that great hope.

—SUSANNA FOTH AUGHTMON

FAITH STEPS: *Journal about your dreams, adding dates for future reference. Know that Jesus is the One who deals in the impossible and is moving on your behalf even now.*

WEDNESDAY, DECEMBER 6

For unto us a child is born, unto us a son is given: and the government shall be upon his shoulder: and his name shall be called Wonderful, Counsellor, The mighty God, The everlasting Father, The Prince of Peace. Isaiah 9:6 (KJV)

WE WERE GATHERED WITH MY husband's family one Christmas when our first child was just a toddler. We had placed a baby crib in the bedroom where we slept, thinking our child would fall asleep quickly. We were mistaken! Our daughter was so excited and filled with the "wonder" of Christmas that she refused to go to sleep. Finally around three or four in the morning, she whimpered her last objections and settled in for a short winter's nap.

I love how children view Christmas. How different our lives would be if we saw life through the lens of a child.

We could start by realizing how God created us. Psalm 139:14 (KJV) says "we are fearfully and wonder-fully (my own spelling) made." Not only that, we can observe how our world is filled with the wonders God has done. Psalm 40:5 says there are too many to declare!

But we celebrate the most wonder-full thing of all at Christmas. Prophesied by Isaiah, he said the child to be born would be called "Wonderful." Jesus, the Son of God, born in a tiny manger!

When I think about the wonder of that first Christmas—the glory of it all—and how thoroughly God prepared for that event, I'm tempted to lose a little sleep myself, especially on the eve of His birthday.

This year, I'm reminding myself at Christmas—and all year long—that life with Jesus is indeed wonder-full. And I'm praying God will give me childlike eyes to always keep it that way.
—REBECCA BARLOW JORDAN

FAITH STEP: *This year, set aside time to look up some of the wonder-full names for Jesus you can find in this passage from Isaiah—and throughout the Bible.*

WEDNESDAY, DECEMBER 6

---

*She will give birth to a son, and you are to give him the name Jesus,
because he will save his people from their sins.* Matthew 1:21 *(NIV)*

WE'D SPENT THE MORNING UNPACKING holiday decorations and hanging them on the tree. As I stepped back to view the finished product, memories warmed me from the inside out. My husband and I exchanged smiles. It was time to set up the crèche—our favorite way to welcome Christmas. Our nativity is extensive, made up of close to thirty pieces. One by one, we unwrapped the white porcelain forms, placing them in a rough arrangement. We had more than half of the boxes emptied when I began to worry.

I didn't see the container holding baby Jesus anywhere. I pushed the collector's boxes back and forth, searching. "Where's the Holy Child?" Panic tinged my voice. My husband pointed to a coffee table where he'd set the piece aside. I blinked and took a deep breath. It was as if I'd been jostled awake, thoughts crowding my mind and emotions.

What if God hadn't decided to redeem us? What if an obedient virgin hadn't accepted the terrible and marvelous honor of motherhood? And most important, what if there hadn't been a baby Jesus? I shuddered.

But Jesus was with God in the beginning and will be with us forever, to the end of the age. My soul finds peace in that promise. For today, I gaze at this tiny figurine that represents our Lord's humble entry into the chaos of our world. Once again, I experience the wonder of a second chance, the vast and eternal hope represented in His birth. And I sigh.

I know how the story ends—happily ever after—for every believer. And I offer a prayer of thanks. —HEIDI GAUL

FAITH STEP: *Spend a few minutes today thinking about what your life would be like if Jesus had never been born. Invite someone over for coffee and give thanks in celebration.*

Thursday, December 7

When Jesus spoke again to the people, he said, "I am the light of the world. Whoever follows me will never walk in darkness, but will have the light of life." John 8:12 (NIV)

Thinking of Jesus as light is an image I can appreciate. I live way out in the country where I find myself in the dark a lot. There are no other houses around—my parents and brother live on either side of me but through the woods—and we are far from the road. No streetlights. No lights from businesses or cars. We're pretty isolated.

Don't get me wrong, I like it. I like to go outside at night and look up in the sky and see total blackness dotted by diamonds. I like to call my mom and tell her to turn on her porch light because I'm on the way down the path. I like to see the sun rise out of the darkness, competing with no other light. I like to watch fireflies sparkle on an otherwise dark landscape.

The thing about darkness is that it amplifies the light. Stars aren't nearly as bright when you're in a city surrounded by lights. And porch lights in a neighborhood, while friendly, don't serve a serious purpose. Even the sunrise is anticlimactic in a place of artificial light.

American novelist Edith Wharton said, "There are two ways of spreading light: to be the candle or the mirror that reflects it." In our relationship with Jesus, He's the candle. We are the mirror that reflects His light to the world. The deeper the darkness, the brighter we shine. —Gwen Ford Faulkenberry

---

Faith Step: *Remember that song you learned as a child, "This Little Light of Mine"? Sing it. Go ahead, you know you want to. Sing it like you mean it.*

THURSDAY, DECEMBER 7

A gift opens the way and ushers the giver into the presence of the great.
Proverbs 18:16 (*NIV*)

CHRISTMAS STOCKINGS HAVE ALWAYS BEEN a big deal on my side of the family. *Who doesn't love a big sock full of tiny treasures to dig into on Christmas morning?* One of my favorite stories about my mom's childhood was her overnight trip from Portland, Oregon, to Modesto, California, after church on Christmas Eve. Driving through the night to reach their grandparents' house, she and her four siblings woke up Christmas morning to find treat-filled stockings hung in each of the car windows. Wonder and laughter abounded. It was a golden moment.

I have continued the tradition with my boys, filling their stockings with chocolate, fun gadgets, and silly socks. I love hearing their laughter when they pull out their gifts. This year as I fill their stockings, I will be looking to find special treats for each one: drawing pencils for Will, remote control gadgets for Addie, and good fiction for Jack. I want to see that look of joy on their faces as they empty their stockings—the look that shows they feel known and loved.

Jesus is the best Giver of gifts. He knows us inside and out. He knows what we need, what we long for, and the things that will fulfill our hearts' desires. In the Psalms, it says He satisfies our desires with good things so that our youth is renewed like the eagle's (Psalms 103:5, NIV). Good gifts are restorative. He pours His goodness out upon us, supplying our every need. In the presence of His love, wonder and laughter abound. —SUSANNA FOTH AUGHTMON

FAITH STEP: *Invite family and friends to fill stockings with special treats. In the spirit of Jesus, deliver them to a homeless shelter, showing those staying there that they are known and loved.*

THURSDAY, DECEMBER 7

But Jesus called the children to him and said, "Let the little children come to me, and do not hinder them, for the kingdom of God belongs to such as these. Truly I tell you, anyone who will not receive the kingdom of God like a little child will never enter it." Luke 18:16–18 (NIV)

EVERY YEAR, JUST FOR FUN, my daughter and son-in-law give me a new toy. I've received water pistols, kaleidoscopes, and paints. These small gifts keep the wonder inside me alive. This year my present was a bottle of bubbles—the kind with a wand you blow through. As I watch those translucent orbs float through the air, I'm able to see my surroundings through the fresh eyes of a child. For a few moments, I regain the ability to look at everything as if for the first time. The thrill of Jesus's creation fills me with a bright perspective.

Jesus loved children. As the creator of all things (John 1:3), He understood their spark of excitement as they encountered new experiences in daily life. The innocence and exuberance kids show over the simplest of pleasures must have delighted Him.

Bringing—and maintaining—this sense of awe in my faith is important to both Jesus and me. To receive His kingdom, I must enter with the trust, hope, and humility of a small child. Revisiting familiar Bible stories with the curiosity of my youth, I find the characters and circumstances coming alive as if I'd never heard them before. New insights bless me.

On days when I feel empty and lost, I run to Jesus and climb into His lap. There's no place safer, nothing more comforting than resting in His care as I pray. I can trust in His love and acceptance today, tomorrow, and always. —HEIDI GAUL

FAITH STEP: *Buy yourself a toy and let it reawaken the child in you. Apply that fresh perspective to your relationship with Jesus. His lap is empty and waiting.*

FRIDAY, DECEMBER 8

"I, the Lord, have called you in righteousness; I will take hold of your hand. I will keep you and will make you to be a covenant for the people and a light for the Gentiles, to open eyes that are blind, to free captives from prison and to release from the dungeon those who sit in darkness." Isaiah 42:6–7 (NIV)

I USED TO THINK CHRISTMAS was all about joy, hope, and peace on earth. I stayed away from reading news stories filled with pain and despair. But the older I get, the more I realize that Christmas may have more to do with chaos than anything else. Because the people of this earth, in a million different ways, are sitting in the dark, afraid. Hoping beyond hope that someone will protect them, hold them, keep them safe, and lift them out of their fear. We have been in desperate need of a Savior. You and I and our families and the billions of others dotting the globe.

Jesus hears our cries. He sees us all. And He is working out His plan. At great detriment to Himself, Jesus came into the darkness of this world. He saw us down in our fears, our pain, our sin, and our despair. And cracked the sky with His light and great love and said, "I am here with you in the middle of this mess. And even better, if you just hold on to me, I will save you."

Knowing we are not alone, that we are caught up in His love and light, and that He came to save us? That is life-altering-hope-filled-we-will-never-be-the-same-again kind of news that we celebrate with great joy at Christmas and all year round. —SUSANNA FOTH AUGHTMON

FAITH STEP: *Light a candle and pray for those in the world who need Jesus in the midst of their darkness to bring them hope and joy this holiday season.*

Friday, December 8

But the Lord answered her, "Martha, Martha, you are anxious and troubled about many things, but one thing is necessary. Mary has chosen the good portion, which will not be taken away from her." Luke 10:41–42 (ESV)

SOMETIMES AN UNWANTED BUT FAMILIAR guest shows up in my home for the holidays. Her name is Anxiety. And she just doesn't show up in my home. Recent research shows an increase in anxiety, especially for women, during the holidays. This is because women usually bear the burden of shopping, cooking, decorating the home, entertaining, and all the other demanding details required to create a meaningful experience for our friends and families. I sure do.

Most of us are familiar with the story of Mary and Martha (Luke 10:38–42). Remember when Martha invites Jesus into her home? And wherever He went, crowds followed. I imagine Martha frantically ran around her home, getting food and water for all the guests. She served those who needed help, cleaned up messes, and probably fluffed pillows so all could be comfortable. Meanwhile Mary lounged on the floor at Jesus's feet, soaking up His every single word. Martha complained to Jesus about her sister not helping, and Jesus gently reminded her that Mary had chosen the good way.

Celebrating the birth of Jesus should be a peaceful experience. He is the Prince of Peace and He longs for us to rest in Him, not be busy because of Him. So this Christmas I challenge you to choose the good way—Mary's example of soaking in the words of Jesus. Celebrate His birth with a heart desiring to know Him. His yoke is easy and His burden is light. Don't have another Martha Christmas—this year have a very "Mary" Christmas. —JEANNIE BLACKMER

FAITH STEP: *Pick a project you planned to do today and don't do it. Instead, prayerfully read Matthew 11:28–30 and experience rest for your soul.*

Friday, December 8

Therefore you do not lack any spiritual gift as you eagerly wait for our Lord Jesus Christ to be revealed. 1 Corinthians 1:7 *(NIV)*

THE CHRISTMAS TREE IS DECORATED, and stockings are hung. Carols waft through the air, joining the scent of holiday baking to create a sense of home and love. And giving.

Every year, I look forward to this season. I enjoy selecting presents that speak to the loved ones in my life, letting them know how much they mean to me. The gratitude I see in their eyes is priceless. And when I give something that's especially dear to me, it makes the moment even more precious.

This Christmas, hidden among the pile of boxes and bags beneath the tree is a tiny package for my daughter. It's a gold ring set with a semiprecious stone I gave my mother long ago. Mom wore it for special occasions until she went to be with Jesus. It's time for me to invite my daughter into the circle of love this bit of jewelry represents. I know she'll cry. I will too.

Long ago, God considered me and my hopeless situation. He saw past my sin and knew exactly what I needed. Surrendering this baby, His Son, would hurt Him more than I can imagine. But He did it so I could enter their circle of love.

Through Jesus, He gave us eternal life and life abundant. It's a gift. Open it. And try not to cry. —HEIDI GAUL

FAITH STEP: *Remember the Gift you were given. What special item can you let go of to welcome someone into your circle of love? If it's a gift, wrap it. If they're words, speak them.*

SATURDAY, DECEMBER 9

Whoever is generous to the poor lends to the LORD,
and he will repay him for his deed. Proverbs 19:17 *(ESV)*

I WAS VERY POOR GROWING up. I lived in a children's home and also was in foster care. One important lesson I learned from that struggle was to be generous to the less fortunate. Jesus placed compassion in my heart for others who suffer… especially children.

When I was a child I received used and broken toys for Christmas. In the unique way that Jesus does things, I am now in charge of a program that provides underprivileged children with new gifts at Christmas. My husband, Clay, and I organize volunteers, set up toy drives, and purchase toys. One lady in our community provides Bibles for the children. High school students have gift drives. Firemen, deputies, and a jolly Santa help deliver the toys, and it's such a blessing to see our community come together to help these beautiful children. Every year before Christmas the other volunteers and I pray Jesus will meet our needs, and He always provides.

Some of the kids' parents feel hopeless when they meet with us, but we minister to them and give them hope. We let them know that we care for them and their children. They are so thankful. And I am so thankful to be able to usher in the joy that I didn't have as a child. The joy I receive from helping these children completely overshadows the bad memories from my childhood.

Acts 20:35 reminds us that it is more blessed to give than receive. Jesus wants us to take care of His kids, both big and little. We can never out-give Jesus, but when we let His generosity pour through us, everyone ends up blessed. —KATIE MINTER JONES

FAITH STEP: *Think of ways you can share your blessings with those who are less fortunate.*

SATURDAY, DECEMBER 9

"You show that you are a letter from Christ, the result of our ministry, written not with ink but with the Spirit of the living God, not on tablets of stone but on tablets of human hearts." 2 Corinthians 3:3 (NIV)

CHRISTMAS LETTERS ARE SUBJECT TO some bad press—teased for their predictable content: a résumé of each child's achievements, a collage of photos of people only vaguely remembered, or glitter-sprinkled tales of "here's what happened this year." I've sent and received each of those over the years. Still, I love Christmas letters. They always speak to me about our human condition.

Whether the letters are full of delightful vacations and career accomplishments, or the somber news of illness and death, they are always scented with a hint of bewilderment. Has another year really gone by already? When did our children grow from cuddly babies into college students? How do we pick up the pieces now that a dear one passed away?

As the letter progresses, that bewilderment often leads to a shift of focus and a beautiful testimony of faith. Yes, the year was full of births and deaths, vacations and layoffs, delights and horrors. Yes, time is grinding past at a relentless pace. But above it all, God is unfolding His plan. For the universe. For our lives.

Life doesn't stand still while we struggle to make sense of it all, so breathing deep of the wonder, confusion and challenges we face is a comfort—as is the reminder that Christ brings meaning to all the ups and downs each year. We are living letters to each other, sharing the beautiful story God is writing with our lives. —SHARON HINCK

FAITH STEP: *Write a letter today, and share a way Christ has written on your life through His Spirit.*

SATURDAY, DECEMBER 9

God, who said, "Let light shine out of darkness," has shone in our hearts to give the light of the knowledge of the glory of God in the face of Jesus Christ. 2 Corinthians 4:6 (ESV)

As a nurse practitioner, I worked twelve-hour night shifts. I drove to work after sunset and followed my headlights home in the morning. I went days without seeing the sun.

I'm grateful I didn't struggle with seasonal affective disorder (SAD) like some of my friends. Our bodies need light and are made to react with sunlight in intricate ways to manufacture vitamin D, which not only helps us to have strong bones, but also plays an important role in preventing and treating disease. I got my vitamin D in capsules during that season.

When the power's out, we bump into furniture and trip over obstacles, fumbling for flashlights and candles. "If you walk in darkness, you don't know where you're going" (John 12:35, MSG). As much as we need light to see and to be healthy, there's one Light we need more.

Prophets from Isaiah to Zechariah spoke of the Light that was coming, not only to shine on us, but *in* us. What love and grace!

Every year during Advent, we light one more candle every week as the darkest days of the year approach, along with Christmas. I love the image of light overcoming gathering gloom as we celebrate the birth of our Savior, announced by angels blazing with brilliance.

Sent because we were lost in the dark. —Suzanne Davenport Tietjen

Faith Step: *Light a candle today during your quiet time. Look up "light" with a concordance and read what Jesus had to say about it.*

PEACE

"Though the mountains be shaken
and the hills be removed,
yet my unfailing love for you will not be
shaken nor my covenant of
peace be removed," says the LORD,
who has compassion on you.

Isaiah 54:10

SECOND SUNDAY OF ADVENT, DECEMBER 10

May you have more and more grace and peace through the knowledge of God and Jesus our Lord. 2 Peter 1:2 *(NIV)*

ONE CHRISTMAS I STEPPED BACK and looked at the tree in our living room. The decorations, lights, tinsel and ornaments looked beautiful. The stockings were hung by the fireplace with care, and festive music boxes adorned the mantel. On one side of the fireplace sat three crudely crafted bottles that had been sprayed and glued with fabric and jewelry years earlier by my children's hands to resemble the Magi.

But as I glanced at the miniature, ivory figures grouped together on the middle of the hearth, I noticed something missing in the small Nativity set. I counted shepherds, Mary and Joseph, sheep, a cow or two, camels, a smaller set of wise men, an angel, the manger, and some straw.

The baby Jesus! Where was Jesus? I searched back through the original box, but found nothing. Somehow, we had lost Jesus.

It wasn't until after Christmas was over, and I was putting things away, that I saw something shiny at the bottom of another Christmas box. Under a wad of paper lay the baby Jesus!

How easy it is to "lose" Jesus in the trappings of busy lives and misplaced priorities. Christmas is not the only time we forget the most important part of life's celebration: Jesus. Without meaning to, we can hide His witness through fear of embarrassment or ignore the most important things in life through simple negligence—any time of year.

That Christmas was a whispered wake-up call to me that Jesus is not only the reason for the season; He is the reason for every day of my life! For me, without Jesus there would be no life, no joy, no peace and no celebration. —REBECCA BARLOW JORDAN

FAITH STEP: *Write a letter to Jesus, thanking Him for what He means to you throughout the year. How can you give Him first place in your life this year?*

SECOND SUNDAY OF ADVENT, DECEMBER 10

*After Jesus was born in Bethlehem in Judea, during the time of King Herod,
Magi from the east came to Jerusalem and asked, "Where is the one who has
been born king of the Jews? We saw his star when it rose and have come to
worship him." Matthew 2:1–2 (NIV)*

LAST NIGHT, I COULDN'T SLEEP. Thoughts swirled in my mind like a
tornado, fractured and chaotic. I rose, walked to the porch and settled into a rocker, waiting for Jesus's peace to calm me. In the darkness, tree limbs swayed to a melody only they could hear. Silence
blanketed the night, and I took a deep breath of the chilled air. My
eyes drifted upward to the stars.

The longer I stared at the sky, the more stars I saw—each one
seeming to sparkle just for me. As I reveled in their distant beauty,
childlike awe welled inside me at the sight of God's vast universe.
Did the wise men experience the same wonder? How could they
have focused on the allure of just one star in a sea of twinkling light?
Because of what it represented to them—a path to the King.

It's been thousands of years since those men made that long journey in search of the Christ child. It couldn't have been easy, yet they
continued their trek until they found Him and honored Him with
gifts. During Christmastime, I can become overwhelmed by a sea of
glittering distractions that lead me away from Jesus. I want to keep
my eyes on the true Star of the season—baby Jesus—and honor
Him. —HEIDI GAUL

FAITH STEP: *The next time the night skies are clear, bundle up and spend some
time outside looking at the stars. As you take in the stellar show, give thanks to the
One who created it.*

SECOND SUNDAY OF ADVENT, DECEMBER 10

*For God so loved the world that he gave his one and only Son, that whoever
believes in him shall not perish but have eternal life. John 3:16 (NIV)*

JACK, OUR OLDEST, IS GETTING ready to go off to college. I remember watching Jack get in line for his first day of kindergarten as if it were yesterday. Dressed in a blue cardigan and tie for chapel, he followed his teacher toward the classroom. Jack looked at me and grinned. I smiled while furiously blinking back tears. There he was. My very heart walking away from me into his amazing future.

Fast-forward to this past week. Jack is staying in California until he leaves for school, while the rest of us move across the country. I went into Jack's room the night before we moved. He was on the floor in a sleeping bag, his bed already loaded for the move. I lay down next to him and began to cry. He patted my back, and I told him, "I love you. I am so proud of you. I am going to miss you like crazy." He grinned at me and said, "I know, Mom. I love you too." Once again, my heart is walking away from me.

What must it have been like for our heavenly Father to send Jesus, His beloved Son, to earth? His very heart leaving the brightness of heaven for earth's darkest reaches. Jesus left His Father for one reason alone: for His love of us. His love is so great, so sacrificial, and so all-encompassing that the magnitude of it is still echoing throughout all of eternity. Our hearts are tended by the One who is love incarnate. In this Advent season, recognize His love for you.
—SUSANNA FOTH AUGHTMON

FAITH STEP: *Turn off the lights and sit in the dark, knowing the brightness of Jesus's love surrounds you this Advent season.*

MONDAY, DECEMBER 11

"For to us a child is born, to us a son is given, and the government will be on his shoulders. And he will be called Wonderful Counselor, Mighty God, Everlasting Father, Prince of Peace." Isaiah 9:6 (NIV)

WHEN MY CHILDREN WERE YOUNG, I sometimes despaired of peace. I'd set the supper table envisioning uplifting conversations about our day, but by the time I'd dished up the casserole, the battles began.

"His chair is too close to mine."

"She got more French fries than me."

"Tell him to stop breathing so loud."

"I get the computer first after supper."

Instead of the grace and love I hoped to instill in my family, my efforts to bring reconciliation and understanding usually resulted in more accusations, cries for justice and pouting.

My frustrating attempts to mediate family squabbles showed me how difficult it is to bring peace. On my own, I couldn't create peace between my children, or peace in my marriage, or even peace within my own thoughts. And I certainly couldn't create reconciliation with God.

Every interaction in my life makes me realize how much I need Jesus, the Prince of Peace. I love this description of the promised Savior in Isaiah. "Mighty" and "Everlasting" reflect His power, and "Counselor" reminds me of His gentle wisdom. Only Jesus has the perfect combination as both God and man to be the Prince of Peace. He's strong enough to solve the problems too big for me, and merciful enough to give His life to restore me. —SHARON HINCK

FAITH STEP: *Is there a lack of peace in an area of your life? An inner conflict, strained relationship or even a barrier in your walk with God? Invite Jesus to be your Prince of Peace, and bring both His power and His love to that situation.*

MONDAY, DECEMBER 11

Do not be overcome by evil, but overcome evil with good. Romans 12:21 (NIV)

MY HUSBAND AND I WERE playing a board game with our son and his family. On one round, my son played a card that caused me to lose points.

"I don't get mad; I get even," I said to him with mock seriousness.

Our five-year-old granddaughter, Anna, overheard. She looked directly in my face and said, "Grandma—getting even isn't right. You must overcome evil with good. That's what Jesus said, so that's the only thing that works."

Wisdom from the mouth of babes. Wisdom from the heart of Christ.

When someone hurts us, our human tendency often wants to get even. But Jesus says not to take revenge. He tells us to treat the offender with respect. If he's hungry, feed him. If he's thirsty, give him a drink. As far as it depends on us, we're to live at peace with everyone (Romans 12:17–20).

Having this attitude isn't difficult—it's downright impossible in our own strength. But the Holy Spirit living in us reminds us of the truth and enables us to obey. Often that means making a deliberate choice to do what we know is right even though our emotions scream otherwise.

Perhaps someone has mistreated you. Ask the Lord for a creative way to demonstrate goodness toward the offender. Don't let evil overcome you, but overcome evil with good. —GRACE FOX

FAITH STEP: *Pray this prayer if someone has hurt you: "Father, help me see this person through Your eyes. Treating him with goodness is impossible in my own strength, so I trust You to empower me to respond in a way that honors You. Amen."*

MONDAY, DECEMBER 11

So if the Son sets you free, you will be free indeed. John 8:36 (NIV)

SOMETIMES CHRISTMAS DOES NOT FEEL like the season of joy and light that it should. Sometimes Christmas feels like a giant snowball of expectations and activities that roars in the Friday after Thanksgiving and doesn't roll out until the new year has been rung in. If we aren't careful, it can squash us flat. I have ordered Christmas cards, purchased Christmas presents for my family, organized the Advent calendar, decorated the house, bought the tree, decorated the tree, marched in a Christmas parade, and gotten Christmas packages together for our kiddos we sponsor in Africa. And I am exhausted. If you need me, I will be in bed until January.

Maybe you have also been squashed by the Christmas snowball. (I may have picked you up when I was rolling down the mountain of bills I was paying yesterday . . . sorry about that.) But here is the thing. Almost none of these activities that are flattening me or you are really Christmas. They are all the trappings we have added to Christmas.

We don't need more parties, or decorations, or gifts, or worries, or expectations to be added to Christmas. What we really need is some grace. For ourselves and others. And we need to love people. My husband just told me that all of us need at least eight hugs a day. He read it somewhere. It sounds about right. And mostly, we need to remember Jesus. Jesus. The Savior. Emmanuel. Breath of Heaven. Redeemer. Bright and Morning Star. Friend. He loves us. There is nothing snowballish about Him. He came so that we could be free . . . not flattened. So breathe.

Grab some grace and spread it around. Hug somebody. And remember that the Light of the World loves you. Completely. Wholly. Without reservation. And that is the real Christmas.
—SUSANNA FOTH AUGHTMON

FAITH STEP: *Repeat the names of Jesus out loud, slowly, pondering their meaning and letting the knowledge that He loves you completely penetrate your heart.*

TUESDAY, DECEMBER 12

"Therefore, since we have been made righteous through his faithfulness combined with our faith, we have peace with God through our Lord Jesus Christ." Romans 5:1 (CEB)

I HATE TO ADMIT THIS, but sometimes I nag God. Like an insistent mosquito buzzing in his ear, I whine and complain about my life. Ironically, one of the things I insistently ask for is peace.

By peace, though, I typically mean that I'd like Him to take care of things that are not easy for me, to change the behavior of people who annoy me, to get rid of my struggles.

Which probably just makes Him laugh. Jesus never promised an easy life; in fact, He told us we'd have troubles. But we can be at peace in the midst of those troubles because when our faith collides with His faithfulness, we're "made righteous" with God. He sees us differently. The things that would disrupt our relationship are gone. It is this unhindered relationship, not our circumstances, that gives us peace.

I'm learning to live in the *peace* that already exists in that relationship, and to pray for peace—not to erase conflict, but peace that will equip me to cope with less than ideal situations.

The word *peace*, which appears in all but two of the books in the New Testament, is most often used as a greeting: grace and peace to you! It describes not just an absence of conflict but harmonious relationships, and the contentment that comes from that relationship.

Jesus is the source of peace for our souls, and for our world. When we have peace in our hearts, we can be peacemakers in the world.
—KERI WYATT KENT

FAITH STEP: *Do you have peace with God through Jesus? If you have put your faith in Him, you do, even if you don't feel it all the time. What do you need to do today to live in that peace?*

TUESDAY, DECEMBER 12

Glory to God in the highest, and on earth peace, good will toward men.
Luke 2:14 (KJV)

THE ANGELS COULD HAVE SAID anything. There was no protocol to follow that night, no script. In fact, if you think about the story of Jesus's birth, there's nothing conventional about it. Two teenagers make a rigorous trip to Bethlehem, as the law dictates, and have a baby in a barn. Shepherds sleeping out in the field to protect their sheep are roused by a bunch of angels. There are so many, they light up the night sky. And even though all the carols claim they were singing, the Bible says the angels were praising God and *saying*, "Glory to God in the highest, and on earth peace, good will toward men."

Think about it. This was the first thing anyone else besides Mary and Joseph had said about Jesus. *Glory to God.* This seems obvious. But the next part is what I find interesting. *And on earth peace and good will toward men.*

This is what the angels celebrated, what they understood as the purpose of Jesus. What His birth did on high was bring glory to God. And for earth? The birth of Jesus meant peace. Good will toward men.

Frederick Douglass said, "I know there is a hope in religion; I know there is faith and I know there is prayer about religion and necessary to it, but God is most glorified when there is peace on earth and good will toward [all people]." I think he was right. If we pay attention to the angels, we'll be about the things Jesus came here for: peace and good will toward all. —GWEN FORD FAULKENBERRY

FAITH STEP: *Make a list of the things you do with Jesus as your motivation. Cross off anything that doesn't promote peace and good will toward all people. Then add things that do as He brings them to mind.*

TUESDAY, DECEMBER 12

When he came, he announced the good news of peace to you who were far away from God and to those who were near. —*Ephesians 2:17 (NIV)*

THE JEWISH PEOPLE OF JESUS's day who lived under the tyranny of Rome longed for when real peace—true cessation of enemy control—would come. And that's what they thought when they heard Isaiah's prophecy of a soon arriving Prince of Peace.

Naturally when Jesus was born, they thought He would usher in that peace. Hadn't the angelic message heard by some shepherds included the words, "Peace on earth, and good will toward men?" But the events that followed didn't measure up for many people. Only those who understood the real peace that Jesus came to bring experienced it. But they did so in their hearts, and it wasn't necessarily reflected in their government.

Is it really any different today? I long for wars to cease around the world and for confused and burdened lives to grasp the only kind of peace that lasts. It won't come from our government or from world leaders. "It" already came over two thousand years ago. "It" was—and is—Jesus (Ephesians 2:14). This Prince of Peace is the One Who made it possible for us to know true peace—not a temporary cease-fire—but a permanent truce with God. Only through Jesus can we find both peace with God—a joyful, loving relationship with Him—and the peace of God, the kind of reassurance that puts complete trust in Jesus (Philippians 4:7). Christmas is a great place to begin to understand that kind of lasting peace.
—REBECCA BARLOW JORDAN

FAITH STEP: *Has Jesus's peace found a place in your heart? If so, write a letter expressing how much that peace means to you. Leave it under the tree for Jesus.*

WEDNESDAY, DECEMBER 13

I know how to live on almost nothing or with everything. I have learned the secret of living in every situation, whether it is with a full stomach or empty, with plenty or little. Philippians 4:12 (NLT)

I FOUND A SCENTED CANDLE for our living room in a home store the other day. I got in line behind a mom and her little girl. The line to the register wound its way through a maze of goodies displayed on either side. The girl asked, "Mom, can I have these fruit chews?"

"No, we are not getting any candy."

Moments later she asked, "Mom, can I get nail polish?"

"No."

"How about this pillow with an *E* for Emma?"

"No, we aren't buying anything else."

This little girl wanted something more. She kept asking. With each step, I grew more impressed with her mom. Finally, when we got to the register, I leaned forward and said, "Good job! I also want to buy everything that I see here."

The lady laughed. She said, "It is hard to say no!"

We never like to hear *no* in life. We want so much. It is easy to grow discontented. We want more talent or a better career or a different relationship. We find ourselves asking Jesus, "Can I have this? What about this? Or this?" Sometimes, Jesus says no. But He promises to give us all that we need for life in this moment. He can grant us grace to be content right where we are. It is not wrong to ask Jesus for more, but peace pours in when we are able to look at the life we have been given with contentedness and gratitude.
—SUSANNA FOTH AUGHTMON

FAITH STEP: *In what area of your life do you struggle to be content? Ask Jesus to show you how to be grateful in this season of your life, knowing that He will provide for your every need.*

WEDNESDAY, DECEMBER 13

The peace of God, which surpasses all understanding, will guard your hearts and your minds in Christ Jesus. Philippians 4:7 (ESV)

WHEN HOPE BREAKS THROUGH DARKNESS, we taste the peace of Jesus that passes understanding. If hope is the light that inspires us to take the chance and believe Jesus is who He claims and follow His sure lead into the future, then peace may just be hope's calming by-product.

Philippians 4:6, coming immediately before today's verse, says, "Do not be anxious about anything, but in everything by prayer and supplication with thanksgiving let your requests be made known to God." That verse speaks of hope—when we hope, we pray and reject anxiety.

Then comes peace.

At times I've been comforted in the calm of the Advent season while I prayed through a concern until His peace settled me.

But peace isn't just passive; it's also a defender. Jesus's peace that passes understanding is a power-packed arsenal against the uncertainties in our lives so that we don't have to be derailed by the troubles that do come up. We don't have to worry about whether we'll have peace next week or beyond this holy season; Jesus is already there, setting up His defenses in and around us. Our faith is strengthened and grown through *peace* that follows in the light created by hope.

This second week of Advent, peace can be yours and mine. But it must be maintained by drawing close to Jesus for security, by turning our minds to Him, who is our hope. In Him our thoughts are guarded, our thoughts that play a mighty role in our level of peace.

—ERIN KEELEY MARSHALL

FAITH STEP: *Buy a gingerbread house kit, and decorate it as a fortress. With icing, write* Peace *across the roof or on the door. Throughout the Advent season, remember that drawing close to Jesus keeps us in His fortress of peace.*

WEDNESDAY, DECEMBER 13

Even the sparrow has found a home, and the swallow a nest for herself, a place near your altar, Lord Almighty, my King and my God. Psalm 84:3 (NIV)

WE TAILORED OUR DECORATIONS THIS year: lighted tree, mantel and hearth, a wreath on the door, and a Nativity scene in the front yard. I fashioned the wreath on the door years ago, so it has endured multiple Christmas seasons in all kinds of Texas weather. Though aged, it still cradles a host of Christmas cheer with its smiling gold angel, burgundy ribbon, and a variety of Christmas symbols.

This season we've already experienced unusual days with record low temperatures. An icy storm left huge tree limbs downed and dangling across property, streets, and power lines. Our huge oak trees, still dressed in the orange and gold leaves of fall, sat with their heavy, icy arms drooping almost to the ground, some laying across the roof.

I wondered how this storm had upset the homes of our neighborhood birds. One morning we opened the front door and noticed something fly out of the wreath. This happened several days in a row. Finally we realized a bird had found a warm, comfy spot and taken up residence in the simple circular "branches" of our Christmas door wreath.

That incident reminded me of Jesus's tender care for all His creation, including us, through all kinds of inclement weather. But more than that, I saw Jesus, the Son of God, a Babe, resting in the simple but warm "nest" of an animal trough that cold, wintry Christmas night. God's eternal love, wrapped in a blanket, the King of kings would soon become the peaceful resting place for our seeking souls: a home near His heart forever.

We, too, can nestle in His wreath of love—an eternal provision for His children. —REBECCA BARLOW JORDAN

FAITH STEP: *If any birds visit your yard, take time to feed them. Then thank Jesus for His eternal love and provision for you.*

THURSDAY, DECEMBER 14

Grace, mercy, and peace, which come from God the Father and from Jesus Christ—the Son of the Father—will continue to be with us who live in truth and love. 2 John 1:3 (NIV)

MY UNCLE JOHN USED TO have a saying that he would ask my cousins and me every time we got antsy in church. As we wiggled, he would whisper, eyes twinkling, "Are you nervous in the service?" We usually were. It was really hard to sit still and pay attention when we had other things on our minds. I still get "nervous in the service." Just yesterday, I got antsy when things didn't go the way I thought they should. I get stressed about bills, raising kids, sticky relationships, and my friends getting cancer. Life often feels too big for me to handle. Jesus looks at my fretful mind and whispers, "Sue, are you nervous in the service?"

Jesus is inviting me and you to a place of peace. He is asking us to trust Him completely with our every concern and desire. He is the Prince of Peace. He reigns over our hearts. Nerves, worries, anxiety, and fear are not found in His kingdom. He asks us to simply talk to Him about our concerns. He wants us to share our thoughts with Him. The good, the bad, and the ugly. And He says if we will turn over our cares to Him with a thankful heart, then He will blow our minds with His unfathomable peace. That peace will hold our hearts and minds in a place of safety. In this Advent season, let the peace of Jesus invade your life. —SUSANNA FOTH AUGHTMON

FAITH STEP: *Share your burdens with a close friend. Ask them to join you in prayer and invite the peace of Jesus into your present situation.*

THURSDAY, DECEMBER 14

Friends, this world is not your home, so don't make yourselves cozy in it.
1 Peter 2:11 (MSG)

FOR THE LAST FEW WINTERS, stray cats have found their way to our back porch. This year was no different—except one day, an entire family showed up.

On a cold morning in December, we looked at the back patio and saw a black mama cat with her four multicolor kittens, all snuggled in our wicker chair. Each time we tried to approach them, they'd run away. But the next night they'd return and sleep until morning. We'd bought new cushions for the chair earlier in the spring, and they must have provided an extra measure of warmth.

I never fed the cats, but still they'd return. Recently, we had to remove the cushions in preparation for some renovations. I remember times when Jesus allowed the cushions in my life to be pulled out from under me, and my safe resting place seemed suddenly scratchy and uncomfortable. In His kind, patient way, Jesus let me know that some renovations were necessary in my life. Would I remain or look for a new shelter in which to place my trust and faith?

I ultimately decided that *home* meant more than a temporary, cozy place on earth. Like the Psalmist, I chose to stay and make the Lord Himself my home (Psalm 73:28, MSG). There, even with uncomfortable renovations, I find not only warmth but safety in the cushion of His love. —REBECCA BARLOW JORDAN

FAITH STEP: *Where do you run when your earthly "home" becomes uncomfortable? Today, rest in Jesus, your real home.*

THURSDAY, DECEMBER 14

Hear this, you leaders of the people. Listen, all who live in the land. In all your history, has anything like this happened before? Tell your children about it in the years to come, and let your children tell their children. Pass the story down from generation to generation. Joel 1:2–3 (NLT)

EVERY DAY LAST WINTER I read a chapter of *The Long Winter* to my youngest kids. My children would use Play Dough or color as I read about Laura Ingalls sleeping in the trundle bed, making snow candy, and watching her pa whisk Ma around the rough-hewn logged dance floor. Sharing this story is like sharing my own childhood and gives me a chance to share important things like home, family, and faith. Their discovery of this young girl's adventures was mine.

As a mom there is so much I want to pass on to my children, yet children don't learn with long lectures or three-point lessons. They learn best when parents share what is meaningful to them. This is true in life. This is true in faith. Just as I share meaningful fictional stories and my kids pay attention, they pay attention when I share meaningful Bible stories too. As I tell them about how Jesus calmed the storm, I also describe how He has brought peace to my life. As I share about David fighting Goliath, I talk about how Jesus gives us strength to face our fears.

When we pass along meaningful stories of Jesus, they become lights within our children's hearts. Lights that may flicker but do not go out. Lights that will warm our children even in the long winters of their own lives. —TRICIA GOYER

FAITH STEP: *Think about a meaningful Bible story. How has that story influenced your life? Now find someone with whom you can share that story and the meaning.*

FRIDAY, DECEMBER 15

The Lord gives his people strength. The Lord blesses them with peace.
Psalm 29:11 (NLT)

I PLACED MY FAITH IN Jesus Christ for salvation when I was eight years old. His presence in my life has blessed me with a gift many people only dream about—inner peace.

This reality struck home while I was on a flight from Seattle to Minneapolis. During the trip, the young woman seated next to me asked what I did for a living. "I'm an inspirational speaker and author," I said.

"Really?" she responded. "I've always wanted to write a book."

"What would you write?" I asked. "What's on your heart?"

The woman paused. Then she answered, "Perhaps I could write about a personal quest. I'm looking for peace. Have you found it?" My jaw nearly dropped. I shot an arrow prayer heavenward asking for the right words. Then I told this young professional about Jesus, the Prince of Peace, and how He desires a relationship with us. I also told her a couple of stories about challenges I've faced and how peace replaced fear in their midst because Jesus gave me wisdom, courage, and perseverance. Our conversation continued with the woman asking several probing questions, ending only when the plane landed.

That encounter helped me understand that peace is not to be taken for granted. Jesus said, "I am leaving you with a gift—peace of mind and heart. And the peace I give is a gift the world cannot give. So don't be troubled or afraid" (John 14:27).

The world is filled with hurting people longing for inner peace and looking in all the wrong places. Let's point them toward Jesus, the Prince of Peace, so their longing can be satisfied. —GRACE FOX

FAITH STEP: *People longing for inner peace surround us. They're our neighbors, coworkers, grocery-store clerks, kids' teachers, and so many more. Ask the Lord to give you the opportunity to tell someone about the Prince of Peace this week.*

FRIDAY, DECEMBER 15

Let the peace of Christ rule in your hearts, since as members of one body you were called to peace. And be thankful. —Colossians 3:15 *(NIV)*

MY SIX-YEAR-OLD DAUGHTER, ADELAIDE, INHERITED the decorating gene from me when it comes to holidays. She and I were ready to put up the Christmas tree at the end of October. It took us until close to Thanksgiving to get our elf-helpers into the mood. Finally, the tree was assembled by a brawnier elf than ourselves, and the village was lit by one a bit more technically inclined. And although Harper no longer put up his tree with the cowboy ornaments, and Grace declined the *Tale of Three Trees* display I offered for her desk, Adelaide happily decked out every square inch of her room with Christmas cheer.

Unfortunately, Adelaide also inherited my gene for clutter. When she showed me her room, I complimented her tree and the reindeer antlers that adorned her stuffed animals. But her dresser was a hodgepodge of snow globes, Santas, snowmen, and ornaments.

"You know what is my favorite, Mommy?"

I couldn't imagine, since I was unable to focus on any one thing.

"It's this one with the sweet little Baby Jesus."

She pointed to a tiny painted pewter Nativity I'd had since I was a child. It's so small that I hadn't even spotted it in the midst of everything else. Adelaide had placed the manger in the center, and Mary and Joseph, the shepherds, and all of the little animals were squeezed around it, as close as they could get.

"See, they are all looking at Him."

And so they were. In the midst of a crazy, cluttered, Christmas extravaganza, Adelaide had created a space for stillness. A place for peace. —GWEN FORD FAULKENBERRY

FAITH STEP: *As the Christmas season cranks up around you, create a peaceful place where you can sit and contemplate Baby Jesus.*

FRIDAY, DECEMBER 15

The Word became flesh and made his dwelling among us. . . . John 1:14 (NIV)

GOD TOOK GREAT CARE TO prepare for Jesus's birth. Throughout the Old Testament, the prophets spoke of the One who would come and reign as King. Isaiah explicitly prophesied Jesus's first coming. He even announced Jesus's royal titles: "Wonderful Counselor, Mighty God, Everlasting Father, Prince of Peace" (Isaiah 9). From Genesis to Malachi, God prepared the way for Jesus's entrance.

But God didn't stop there. He kept on preparing: a young woman named Mary who would bear His Son through miraculous birth; the shepherds, who would see and hear the angels' announcement, and be the first to see the newborn; a prophetess named Anna and a devout man named Simeon, who also witnessed the fulfillment of God's promise.

The wise men followed a star, prepared long ago to guide them to Jesus at just the right time, and then came John the Baptist, the gritty desert dweller destined to prepare the way for Jesus's coming.

Even before our birth, God prepared a special place for Jesus to be "born again" in us—not physically, but spiritually. That's when we can celebrate *both* birthdays all year long: ours and our Savior's.

Christmas is so much more than a holiday. It's even more than the birthday of Jesus. The true spirit of Christmas begins the moment we invite the Lord Jesus into our hearts. And it lasts more than just a day or a season. That spirit keeps on going and going.

The Word that became flesh through Jesus now lives in us. How exciting that now, after Jesus's birth, death and Resurrection, Jesus continues the preparations God began—this time for His glorious coming again. —REBECCA BARLOW JORDAN

FAITH STEP: *As you make your preparations for Christmas this year, remember to prepare your own heart in grateful celebration for the One who wants to live in every person.*

SATURDAY, DECEMBER 16

"To give light to those who sit in darkness and in the shadow of death, and to guide us to the path of peace." Luke 1:79 (NLT)

As NOVEMBER TURNED TO DECEMBER, I created a playlist of favorite Christmas songs that accompanied any car travel, housework, and sometimes computer work as I prepared my heart for a Jesus-centered holiday.

A handful of songs rose above the rest. More than atmosphere-setters, they became part of the illumination of the season for me. I hit "replay" over and over and let the Holy Spirit use the music to pry my heart open wider for the celebration of Christ's birth. One of those songs has a title not instantly connected with Christmas classics: "All Is Well." But in some ways, it defines the message of Christmas.

The year I most appreciated the song, everything seemed anything but "well" in our household. Personal messages from friends told of family crises, rough diagnoses, breath-stealing challenges. And in our own home, we were approaching the date predetermined for my husband's company's downsizing, which meant the end of his job.

Against that backdrop came the song "All Is Well." As soon as the last note ended, I hit "replay." I needed to hear it again. It turned into a prayer of gratitude that Jesus came to our messy world to let us know it would get even messier, but we could still know deeply embedded peace. The poetry of the lyrics found their footing in the truth foretold in ancient times in anticipation of the arrival of Jesus on the scene: "For tonight darkness fell / Into the dawn of love's light."

Circumstances have no power against the relentless "dawn of Love's light," against the unstoppable presence of Jesus, the Light of the world. —CYNTHIA RUCHTI

FAITH STEP: *This Advent season, inscribe your "darkness" concerns into the wax of a pillar candle. As you burn that candle each evening, watch those concerns melt as the light—the Light—takes over.*

SATURDAY, DECEMBER 16

But you, Bethlehem Ephrathah, though you are small among the clans of Judah, out of you will come for me one who will be ruler over Israel, whose origins are from of old, from ancient times. Micah 5:2 (NIV)

IN OUR HOME, BY THE second Sunday in Advent, we usually have our decorations up, and the excitement for Christmas is building. We gather around the Advent wreath and light the "Bethlehem Candle." The light grows as Christ's birth draws nearer.

This candle reminds us of Mary and Joseph's obedient response to God, as well as their trip to Bethlehem. I hated to travel when I was pregnant, so I always pause to admire Mary's journey.

The city of Bethlehem also challenges my thinking. The King of Kings, who has always been, didn't arrive in a capital city with a powerful army. He chose a humble young woman to give Him human birth, in a small town of a small clan in a rough-hewn shelter.

I draw great comfort from this glimpse of our Savior. When I think of the great men and women of the Bible and throughout history, I feel like the least significant among His people. I'm daunted by stories of brave missionaries or the huge accomplishments of leaders of various ministries. He offers to live in our hearts and our lives, but I struggle with doubt. Could Jesus—the Lion of Judah who comes to rule over all—really make His home within me?

Long before His birth, He made clear that His dwelling is with the small and humble and the rough-hewn.

Do you ever feel insignificant? As we light the Bethlehem candle for the second Sunday in Advent, we can take heart. This same Jesus who chose Bethlehem for His arrival chooses us for His own.
—SHARON HINCK

FAITH STEP: *Light the first Advent candle and remember the promises it represents. Then light the second candle and rejoice that Jesus dwells with us.*

SATURDAY, DECEMBER 16

Finally, brothers and sisters, rejoice! Strive for full restoration, encourage one another, be of one mind, live in peace. And the God of love and peace will be with you. 2 Corinthians 13:11 (NIV)

DURING THE CHRISTMAS SEASON, I usually hang a simple marquee sign that lights up the word *PEACE* across our carport. Until this year. When I turned it on, it read *ACE.* I have another marquee sign for the bookcase next to our fireplace that reads *JOY.* It was also losing bulbs. I thought I could change some out and have either *PEACE* or *JOY* instead of *ACE* and *OY.* I switched out the bulbs, but now, neither of them lights up. So I decided that I would buy some new marquee lighting spelling *HOPE.* The letters arrived yesterday. No *H.* Just *OPE.*

This seems to be a reflection of my life. Searching for complete *peace, joy,* and *hope,* but not quite there yet. I think that is where Jesus comes in. Into my brokenness. Our brokenness. With the brightness of His love. The One Who was born in a stable, amid the muck and bellow of animal cries, is used to bringing peace, joy, and hope into our messy lives. He does it with angel choirs and brilliant stars and extravagant gifts. Loving us right where we are. Bringing His glory and holiness when we have none of our own, so that we can stand together, loved and restored. Holding out our hands to the heavens, we can shout, "It's so good that You came!" and "What in the world would we do without You?"

It is because of Jesus and His presence in our lives that, on this cold December evening, we can have truckloads of *OY,* an overwhelming sense of *OPE,* and an all-encompassing blanket of *ACE* on earth, good will toward men. —SUSANNA FOTH AUGHTMON

FAITH STEP: *Step outside into the cold, raise your hands in the air, and thank Jesus for the peace, joy, and hope that He has showered down on your life.*

JOY

But let all who take refuge in you be glad;
let them ever sing for joy.
Spread your protection over them,
that those who love your name
may rejoice in you.

Psalm 5:11

SUNDAY, DECEMBER 17

The shepherds returned, glorifying and praising God for all the things they had heard and seen. Luke 2:20 (NIV)

ON THE THIRD SUNDAY IN Advent, we light the joy or shepherd candle. Although the other candles on the wreath are usually purple or dark blue, the shepherd candle is traditionally pink—a reflection of the joy the shepherds experienced at hearing the Good News.

Just as the Bethlehem candle reminded us that Christ comes to humble places, now we consider the humble shepherds.

Their initial reaction to the angel's proclamation was fear. I have to admit, if I saw a night sky lit with an angel choir, I'm sure I'd tremble. But after they were given the news, they hurried to find the babe—a Good Shepherd come to save these shepherds and all of humanity. They saw Him, and it forever changed them. They spread the word, excited to share the joy. And as they returned to their ordinary lives, they gave glory to God. I'm sure after that night, their daily tasks glowed with a new sense of wonder and hope.

Jesus does more than act in our lives. He invites us to respond. During this Advent season, we can take a cue from the shepherds. We can hear the story with awe. We can draw close to Jesus and look deeply into His life as we read the Scripture and pray. We can share the wonderful news of His coming with others. And as we leave our devotional encounters with our Good Shepherd, we can return to our day glorifying and praising God. —SHARON HINCK

FAITH STEP: *Underline all the verbs in Luke 2:16–20. Think about seeing, spreading the word, glorifying, and praising. Look for ways to carry out the same responses today.*

SUNDAY, DECEMBER 17

"The virgin will conceive and will give birth to a son, and they will call him Immanuel" (which means "God with us"). Matthew 1:23 (NIV)

SOMETIMES IT IS EASY TO lose sight of real joy amidst the glorious holiday cheer and rapidly expanding Christmas card list. We get wrapped up in wish lists and scheduling and two-for-one sales. When really, the whole reason we are celebrating so heartily is because we are no longer trying to navigate life and its problems by ourselves. We are not living life without a purpose, without a hope.

When we peel back the layers of Christmas, when we push past the fourteen and a half trips to the mall, the kid's musicals, the parties and the eggnog, when we peer past the needs for tablets, puffy jackets, shimmery lip gloss and the cool video game, we recognize what we really truly need for Christmas, and for life in general, is to not be alone.

One night, long ago, far from here, Jesus broke through the heavens with an answer. With a purpose. With a person. With himself. A baby. Tiny, squalling, wrapped in cloth, lying in a feed trough. His name is Christ the Lord. Emmanuel.

And like the angels, we can say, Glory to God in the highest. Peace on earth. Goodwill toward men. Because Jesus is with us. And it does not get any more joyful than that. —SUSANNA FOTH AUGHTMON

FAITH STEP: *You are not alone. Jesus's name reminds of this. Read the telling of Jesus's birth in Luke 2:1–40 and remember once again that He came here for you.*

Sunday, December 17

"Think of the various tests you encounter as occasions for joy."
James 1:2 (CEB)

"WON'T *THIS* BE AN ADVENTURE!" my friend said, noting that the lights had gone out not only in our rental condo but all over the city, judging from the darkened landscape we could see through the window.

Some complain when the lights go out, but my friend was curious about the adventure we'd have because of it. That was her response to most things other people might find irritating or disruptive.

She wasn't out of touch with reality. On the contrary, she was deeply in touch with the reality Jesus came to bring. He told us His joy could be ours (John 15:11). His Word says that His joy is our strength—and why would that matter if we weren't constantly desperate for strength?—and that we can "count it all joy" when trouble comes (James 1:2). Consider those challenges "occasions for joy," as the Common English Bible puts it. *Adventures.*

James 1:2 is a verse that can evoke confusion, disbelief, or anger for some. Joy? Out of a disheartening situation? That doesn't even make sense…unless you understand that because of the intense love of Jesus, we can trust His assurance that even the things we suffer make us more complete individuals (James 1:3–4). The process doesn't have to empty us. It can make us full because of the presence of Jesus made more tangible than ever in our time of need.

In that light, at times life feels like an amusement park with too many rides. But our hearts not only beat faster, they're stronger when we reach the adventure's end. —CYNTHIA RUCHTI

FAITH STEP: *Have you logged your current situation into the "Occasions for Joy" column yet? You can reframe an aspect of today's trial as "Adventure with Jesus." See what happens.*

MONDAY, DECEMBER 18

Rejoice always, pray continually, give thanks in all circumstances; for this is God's will for you in Christ Jesus. 1 Thessalonians 5:16–18 (NIV)

RECENTLY I WROTE A STORY about a young girl at our gym named Kathryn. Not long after she learned about the story and her mother read it to her, my husband came home from work with a card for me. The outside of the card had, in adorable block letters, *Mrs. J.R.*

The mere way that she addressed the envelope made me smile, but when I opened it, the message on her card melted me. It read, "Thanks for making me feel so loved." It was signed Kathryn and then followed with a big smiley face.

Too often I have someone do something kind for me, and I forget to let them know how much I appreciate their thoughtfulness. Kathryn didn't forget. She didn't have to make that card for me, but her effort and the sweet message inside gave me much joy.

Paul tells us in the verse above that we are to give thanks in all circumstances. Obviously Kathryn is taking that verse to heart. I plan to do a better job of following through with that command and look for each and every opportunity to say thanks. —RENEE ANDREWS

FAITH STEP: *Buy a pack of eight thank-you notes today. Then strive to send them all within the next eight weeks.*

MONDAY, DECEMBER 18

Then Jesus said to them, "So wherever you go in the world, tell everyone the Good News." Mark 16:15 (GW)

ONE DECEMBER OUR YOUTH PASTOR paid a visit to a church member who'd been hospitalized. As James neared the patient's room, another door at the far end of the hallway opened and a man rushed out. This man ran down the hall, shouting at the top of his lungs, "She's all right! She's all right!" He stopped in front of James, grabbed his shoulders, and repeated his message. Then he continued shouting.

Pastor James never learned the details of this stranger's situation. But it was obvious the man had good news that he wanted to share with everyone. How appropriate that this scenario played out in December, a season when we celebrate the words of an angel to shepherds announcing that the Savior of the world had been born: "I have good news for you, a message that will fill everyone with joy" (Luke 2:10, GW).

As Jesus ascended back to heaven after His resurrection, He instructed His followers to tell everyone the good news about God's kingdom wherever they went (Mark 16:15). While I often fall short in this area, I've decided that December is the perfect time to improve. I will resist the pressure to try to craft the picture-perfect holiday. Instead I will plan activities, choose gifts, and engage in conversations that point toward Jesus and what His life and death made possible: forgiveness of sins, unconditional love, and eternal life. What better time to share the most wonderful news than the most wonderful time of the year? —DIANNE NEAL MATTHEWS

FAITH STEP: *Why not read the book of Luke over the next couple of weeks and ask Jesus to help you share the Good News?*

MONDAY, DECEMBER 18

You know the message God sent to the people of Israel, announcing the good news of peace through Jesus Christ, who is Lord of all. Acts 10:36 (NIV)

GROWING UP, MY FAMILY ALWAYS opened gifts on Christmas Eve. We kids would go into a back bedroom and wait . . . and wait. Finally, we'd hear the *ding-a-ling* of bells, followed by Dad's hearty voice: "Santa has come!" We could always tell the "Santa" gifts. Under the tree sat our fulfilled hopes: a shiny bicycle, a new baby doll, or a fun bake-oven. The anticipation was over. We felt happy and satisfied.

The world awaited another time of expectancy as prophecy after prophecy foretold the coming of One Who would bring love and peace. Centuries of oppression had led to confusion and disappointment. Would the promised One ever come?

And then one starry night as shepherds waited on a hillside, the heavens opened up and an angelic chorus announced that the time of waiting had ended: "Jesus has come!" The hopes and dreams of all the years were fulfilled in the birth of a baby named Jesus. Messiah, Son of God, Redeemer, Christ the Lord.

And as the shepherds followed the angels' instructions and drew near to the babe lying on the bed of hay, they had no doubt that this shining gift was from God. Those who heard the good news and received the gift felt joy and satisfaction.

Over two thousand years have passed, but we who know the Gift and the Giver can share the joyful message: "Jesus has come... and He's coming back again!" —REBECCA BARLOW JORDAN

FAITH STEP: *Think about when you first understood Jesus, God's gift, had come—for you. Ask Him to prepare your heart for the celebration of Christmas.*

TUESDAY, DECEMBER 19

"See what great love the Father has lavished on us, that we should be called children of God! And that is what we are!" 1 John 3:1 (NIV)

IT IS 6:48 AM, THE exact time my children must leave for the bus each morning. I send them off with words, since teenagers rarely tolerate a hug good-bye that early in the day.

"Have a good day," I tell them. "Good luck on your math test. I'll be praying for you."

I watch them, two coltlike blond teenagers in black parkas, their long legs striding down the sidewalk, ready to break into a gallop if they see the bus at the corner. I watch them, still sort of amazed as they move relentlessly toward adulthood and independence.

There's a pull in my heart when I see my kids—whether they are leaving for school, playing sports or hanging out at home. Even when my kids are difficult, I love them. It sometimes overwhelms me.

We are God's children: loved, chosen. His love is extravagant and lavished upon us. We do not have to pry scraps of affection from God's clenched fist. He pours it out with abundance. Because of Jesus, He has adopted us as His own.

The way we love our kids on our best, most unselfish day—that's not even close to how much God loves us, all the time. Now, loving my kids does not mean indulging their every whim. In fact, sometimes love means setting limits, telling them "no."

God's love is much the same—it sustains and holds us. It sometimes sets limits. The struggles of this life do not negate God's love for me, any more than the struggles my children face negate my love for them. —KERI WYATT KENT

FAITH STEP: *Today, spend some time being quiet with God, receiving the love He wants to lavish upon you. Remember that, as His beloved child, you don't have to earn His favor.*

TUESDAY, DECEMBER 19

"The kingdom of heaven is like treasure hidden in a field. When a man found it, he hid it again, and then in his joy went and sold all he had and bought that field. Matthew 13:44 (NIV)

DUE IN PART TO A sixteenth-century mathematician named Johannes Kepler and his discovery of how the solar system works, astronomers and others have been able to actually see with their own eyes what the sky looked like in Jerusalem over two thousand years ago. In fact, they can now calculate the exact positions of all the stars and planets on any date in history.

Before Jesus' birth, some Magi astronomers from the East had apparently been studying those same heavens—the solar system—for years, tracking their prophetic signs. They recognized the Bethlehem Star—"his star"—the perfect, heavenly culmination of God's creative planning that would lead them to the one "born king of the Jews."

Like King Herod, the Magi could have relied on secondhand information and sent someone else to find the babe, Jesus. But they had to see for themselves. Persistently, they journeyed for days, weeks—however long it took to find Him. And when their eyes finally rested on the young child, Jesus, they were overjoyed and bowed down and worshipped Him.

We can tell others about the story of Jesus, where He was born, and who He was, but until they "see" Him for themselves—until they persistently seek Him and find Him personally—they won't experience the same joy.

Because "seeing" Jesus for the first time is always a life-changing moment. —REBECCA BARLOW JORDAN

FAITH STEP: *Do you remember the first time you "saw" Jesus—when you really understood who He was and how much He loved you? Pray for others this Christmas who still need to see Jesus for themselves.*

TUESDAY, DECEMBER 19

"To love him with all your heart, with all your understanding and with all your strength, and to love your neighbor as yourself is more important than all burnt offerings and sacrifices." Mark 12:33

CHRISTMAS IS ALMOST HERE. MANY of us are spending time shopping for gifts for loved ones. Some are baking, some are volunteering, and some are decorating. That's what I'm doing this week. As my husband and I set up our white porcelain Nativity set, my hand rests on one of the wise men. He's traveled a long way and is tired, but he's kneeling before the infant King, a look of deep reverence on his face. He's holding an urn, stretching his arms toward Jesus. The other wise men seem expectant, eager as children to present Him with their treasures. In his bed of straw, Jesus is napping. I sigh as I rearrange a few of the animals and push the wise men closer. This is peace.

Soon we'll begin our family traditions. Baking day is important. As all of us crowd the kitchen, scooping flour and adding extracts, laughter draws us closer. Then we'll handstamp our wrapping paper and tags, stealing an opportunity to slow down and be creative. We'll attend the Christmas Eve candlelight service and share a German apple puff pancake on Christmas morning.

But this year, I want to give Jesus something. Something precious and irreplaceable, something worth more than gold, frankincense, and myrrh. Something beyond tithing and even volunteering. I'm anticipating how much this gift will please Him. Because I plan to give Him *everything* this season. All my hopes, dreams, talents, and trust. All my love. All of me. Every single bit. Just like He did for me. —HEIDI GAUL

FAITH STEP: *You can give everything to Jesus. What have you held back? Give Him every bit of you. That's exactly what He wants!*

WEDNESDAY, DECEMBER 20

Look! The virgin will conceive a child! She will give birth to a son and will call him Immanuel (which means "God is with us"). Isaiah 7:14 (NLT)

MY HUSBAND AND I USUALLY spend part of our Christmas road trip in the town where our sons live, and our daughter's family goes to visit my son-in-law's family. We used to stay at a hotel and meet them at a restaurant for a couple of hours, but two years ago, we decided to rent a house instead of a hotel room. This gave us plenty of space, and I was able to cook for my family. We all agreed it was a better option.

Last year, I found a rental house that looked perfect online. But after driving one thousand miles over two days, we arrived to find that the cleaning crew had not come—and wouldn't be coming. I spent the evening pulling sheets off stained mattresses, washing dirty towels, and cleaning bathrooms. The next day, I bought some household items along with groceries, did prep work for our Christmas meal, and more cleaning. Late that night, I settled down to sleep on the couch since my husband had been sick in bed since the day after we arrived. Suddenly, the doorbell rang. It was a man holding giant packages of toilet tissue, which we didn't need. The next day, as I cleaned up after dinner, the garbage disposal cracked and gushed out water.

The older I get, the more I realize I can't make Christmas perfect for my family. But that's okay. The baby in the manger was called Immanuel because God had come down to earth in human form. If we know Jesus as our Savior, He is still with us, now and forever. And that's enough to make any imperfect holiday perfectly wonderful. —DIANNE NEAL MATTHEWS

FAITH STEP: *Each time you feel stressed about holiday details, take a deep breath and meditate on what "Immanuel, God with us," means to you.*

WEDNESDAY, DECEMBER 20

"For the joy that was set before him endured. . . . " Hebrews 12:2 (ESV)

UNDER THAT UGLY, LINT-MAGNET MAROON carpeting in our dining room lay maple flooring original to this one-hundred-year-old house. When the backing threads began to show through in high-traffic areas years ago, I knew it was time to commit: restore the hardwood or install different carpeting.

I removed the Daily Annoyance Carpet, exposing a layer of linoleum tiles likely dating from the forties. The tiles released their hold reluctantly. Underneath, a black, tarry glue resisted all removal techniques other than me on my knees with a putty knife.

Then sanding. Then removal of evidence of sanding. Then staining. Then a polyurethane coat followed by drying time, sanding, wiping off the residue, another polyurethane coat. Repeat three times.

Now the floor glows with a warm sheen. Worth it? Definitely!

I pressed on because of the promise of a joy-filled end result. In the Bible, we read about what Jesus endured for the joy set before Him. "He endured the cross, ignoring the shame, for the sake of the joy that was laid out in front of him" (Hebrews 12:2, CEB).

What joy? He endured the Cross for the joy of pain relief when He returned to life again? The joy of being freed from the world that misunderstood Him so badly, treated Him so cruelly?

According to the rest of what we read in God's Word, those were secondary to the goal of seeing us restored, affording us the opportunity to shine, our sins forgiven, with unlimited access to the Father God through the Son! *That* joy. He endured the Cross out of love for us. Never-ending relationship with us was the joy-set-before-Him. —CYNTHIA RUCHTI

FAITH STEP: *"I am the joy for which He endured." Say it aloud. Does this reality flood your heart with gratitude? Consider three ways that your life can shine because of what Jesus endured for you.*

WEDNESDAY, DECEMBER 20

Praise be to the God and Father of our Lord Jesus Christ, who has blessed us in the heavenly realms with every spiritual blessing in Christ.
—Ephesians 1:3 (NIV)

LAST YEAR I HAD A different kind of Christmas. I didn't put up a tree. I didn't attend any Christmas plays, musicals, or special events. Didn't wrap a single present or bake a single cookie or mail a single card. Selling your house right after Thanksgiving and then moving across country the week before Christmas puts a big dent in normal celebrating.

Even before the house sold, I had been flying back and forth between two states to visit my husband. Occasionally, I had brief panic-filled moments when I thought, *Oh no! I'm missing Christmas!* Sometimes I felt cheated out of enjoying the things I love about the season. My perspective changed during the long drive to visit loved ones before heading to our new location. Finally, I was forced to slow down as Christmas music on the radio prepared me to celebrate the essence of Christmas instead of its trappings.

Having a Christmas stripped of the usual activities and traditions drew my focus to the real blessings. Instead of having my children and grandchildren over for a homemade feast, we gathered at a steakhouse. I couldn't present all my family members with carefully chosen gifts, but I could shower them with love.

My pared-down version of Christmas left more room for the miracle we celebrate: God coming down to earth in the form of a baby. A love that compelled Jesus to die in our place so we can live forever. Gifts of mercy, forgiveness, and grace freely offered to those who believe. —DIANNE NEAL MATTHEWS

FAITH STEP: *Ask Jesus if you need to strip away anything from your holiday busyness so you can focus more on Him this Christmas season.*

THURSDAY, DECEMBER 21

You will go out in joy and be led forth in peace; the mountains and hills will burst into song before you, and all the trees of the field will clap their hands.
Isaiah 55:12 (NIV)

WHEN SCOTT AND I GOT the news by text from our Realtor that our offer had been accepted on our new home, I had to bust out a few nineties dance moves. Since college, the Running Man has been my dance of choice. Flinging back my head, I pumped my arms, proceeding with a jig of jubilation. Scott started laughing. His laughter wasn't just because of my superior dance skills or the fact that I could keep up the dance for only about seventy-two seconds. It was brought on by his sheer, unadulterated joy. We had been surprised, once again, by the goodness of Jesus—upended by His amazingness. He blessed our socks off. It is what He does.

When Mary learned that she was going to miraculously give birth to the Son of the Living God, she broke out into a hymn of praise about the Lord's goodness. When her cousin Elizabeth, who was living out her own pregnancy miracle, greeted Mary, John the Baptist broke out into his own dance of joy . . . in utero. They were all caught off guard by the promise and presence of Jesus. The Savior. Emmanuel. God with us. Jesus is too wonderful to understand. His ways are too marvelous to behold. He delights in surprising us with His mercy, grace, and love. In the most out of the way places and in the most impossible circumstances, Jesus is always waiting to break into our lives with His goodness. In this Advent season, embrace His joy. —SUSANNA FOTH AUGHTMON

FAITH STEP: *Consider how Jesus surprises you regularly with His goodness. Do a jig of joy in your living room and let that joy fill you up.*

THURSDAY, DECEMBER 21

When they saw the star, they rejoiced with exceedingly great joy. And when they had come into the house, they saw the young Child with Mary His mother, and fell down and worshiped Him. And when they had opened their treasures, they presented gifts to Him: gold, frankincense, and myrrh.
Matthew 2:10–11 (NKJV)

EXCEEDINGLY GREAT JOY. WORSHIP. GIFTS. It's interesting to me to note the progression in these verses as the wise men move closer to Jesus. First, they see the star. Like the sun, it beams joy into their hearts. Joy that their journey is not in vain—they will find what they are seeking. And what about when they reach their destination? The Bible says when they see Jesus, they fall down on their faces and worship, presenting Him with gifts.

In the Church Age it's easy for us to lose the wonder—the joy—of seeing Him. We have crosses on our walls, light-up Nativity scenes, paintings; Adelaide's Sunday school class even has a flannel-graph Jesus. Maybe there was magic when we first received Him into our hearts, but sometimes He becomes too comfortable. We're used to Him. He's a fixture in our lives we take for granted.

There's a beauty in being so secure, so familiar, that we're comfortable with Jesus. I believe on some level He wants us to feel that way. But there's also a lesson for us in the story of the wise men. As we recognize the reward for seeking Him, may our hearts be filled with joy. And as we move closer to the Babe in the manger, let's remember the majesty clothed in His humanity and worship Him. Bring Him our gifts, whatever they may be, that He may use us to build His Kingdom on the earth. —GWEN FORD FAULKENBERRY

FAITH STEP: *Christina Rossetti writes, "What can I give Him, poor as I am? If I were a shepherd, I would bring a lamb. If I were a Wise Man, I would do my part. Yet, what can I give Him: give Him my heart." Give Jesus your heart today.*

Thursday, December 21

"Let your light shine before men, that they may see your good deeds and praise your Father in heaven." Matthew 5:16 (NIV)

I LOVE CANDLES. AT HOLIDAYS and other special times, I enjoy the sweet fragrance of cinnamon, apple or floral smells filling my home. My daughters always know a gift that will please me whenever birthday or Christmas rolls around.

Now they carry on the familiar tradition: Just before company arrives, we usually light a candle. Our ritual does more than hide cooking odors or announce a guest's arrival. It's also a symbol of love that says, "You are special!" "You are loved." "You matter!"

As I read Jesus' words recently about letting our light shine, it reminded me of an Old Testament description of another light.

The high priest Aaron and his sons were given the job of keeping the lamp burning in the Holy Place of the tabernacle all night long (Exodus 27:21). The light in that seven-candled lamp stand was a representation of God's presence—and a foreshadowing of Jesus' coming. The oil, a product of olives beaten and pressed like the Lord Jesus Himself, symbolized the Spirit of the Lord that now burns brightly with hope in the hearts of all believers.

Lighting those candles began to spark an inner desire: that my home and my life would be a symbol to others of the light and hope Jesus brings. I couldn't burn a literal candle all night. But perhaps I could light a candle more often than just during Christmas and other special days.

Because of Jesus' coming, we can let our light shine for Him day and night throughout the year.

I think it's time to go light another candle. —REBECCA BARLOW JORDAN

FAITH STEP: *Place a fragrant candle in a prominent spot, such as on your kitchen table. Each time you light it, say a prayer that Jesus will let your light shine for Him every day.*

FRIDAY, DECEMBER 22

So you have sorrow now, but I will see you again; then you will rejoice, and no one can rob you of that joy. John 16:22 (NLT)

MY FAMILY HAS GREAT MEMORIES from the eight years we lived by a lake. It was where we brought our newborns, and where a winter ice storm knocked out our power for a week when we had a toddler and a seven-week-old baby. The roads were slick, and hundred-year-old trees had snapped under the ice's weight and fallen across the pavement, so we couldn't risk driving back to town. We were stuck.

Before long the "adventure" grew old, and we longed for electricity and warmth and space to stretch out. Trapped far from medical care with two little ones, I felt robbed of my sense of security.

We want the security of knowing what we value is protected and safe, whether people we care about or property we own. We don't often think of our joy being rendered powerless, but how tragic would that be if Jesus didn't secure lasting joy for us! His joy never yields to ice storms or any other disaster.

"The joy that Jesus came to bring is from outside this world. It is the very joy that Jesus himself has in God the Father—which he has had from all eternity and will have forever," writes author Jon Piper. In this third week of Advent, we celebrate the joy Jesus ushered in. Jesus is Immanuel, "God with us," at all times, in all things.

Today we look back with wonder that God came into the world, and we look forward to His return, expecting the great unceasing joy He has promised us, joy that cannot, not ever, be taken away!
—ERIN KEELEY MARSHALL

FAITH STEP: *Look up Romans 15:13 for more on joy. Memorize it and John 16:22.*

FRIDAY, DECEMBER 22

A cheerful heart is good medicine, but a crushed spirit dries up the bones.
Proverbs 17:22 *(NIV)*

LAUGHING IS MY FAVORITE THING to do. I like funny movies. I love funny books. I share funny videos. If someone else starts laughing, I have to join in. We place a high value on humor in our family. I love it when my kids get tickled and break out in giggles. If I can make my husband and kids laugh? I feel like I have won the lottery. The best moment is when my husband, Scott, laughs until he cries. None of us can keep it together when he is laughing that hard.

What is it about joy that is so contagious?

I have a hunch that we love to laugh so much because Jesus created us for joy. His Word is full of joy references, such as *You shall go out with joy and be led forth with peace. Weeping may endure for the night, but joy comes in the morning. In His presence there is fullness of joy. The joy of the Lord is my strength.*

Life can be hard. There is brokenness and grief to contend with. There are dark days in all of our lives. But the truth is that we were formed with joy in mind. Joy heals us and restores us like good medicine. Joy lifts our spirits and ushers in hope. If we can laugh, if we can find joy, even in the dark moments, we know that we are not alone. He is there. The One in whom joy resides. Jesus, with all His hope and goodness and love, is the joy-bringer. Embrace that joy-filled person that He created us to be! —SUSANNA FOTH AUGHTMON

FAITH STEP: *Get together with a joyful friend. Laugh as much as you can and thank your friend for being like Jesus, the joy-bringer.*

FRIDAY, DECEMBER 22

"Now I am coming to you. I told them many things while I was with them in this world so they would be filled with my joy." John 17:13 (NLT)

LIFE HAS ITS UNPLEASANT MOMENTS, but when I think of happy occasions, I remember celebrations from the past: the day I graduated from high school, the day I married, the birth of our children and grandchildren, special birthdays, anniversaries, vacations—and more. The memories bring joy to my heart.

When Luke describes happy occasions involving both the birth of John the Baptist (Luke 1:14) and the announcement of Jesus's birth, he records the angels using the qualifier *great* joy. I've always thought of joy as, well, joy. I found the same words in other passages as well. And most of them referred to a degree of emotion involving the Deity.

Jesus Himself prayed before His death that His disciples would experience the full measure of His joy (John 17:13, NIV). And speaking to His disciples in John 15:11, Jesus told them He wanted His joy to remain in them, that it would be *full*. Other translations use the words *complete joy* or joy that *overflows*. Is it any wonder then that the angels would describe Jesus's birth at Christmas as bringing *great* joy, *complete* joy, *overflowing* joy?

We still experience pain and heartache in this world. But the *great* joy that Jesus brings remains embedded in our hearts, ready to explode in celebration when we see Him face-to-Face.

At that moment, every believer who has ever known Jesus, will experience a complete and lasting joy. —REBECCA BARLOW JORDAN

FAITH STEP: *Thank Jesus for happy moments and celebrations in your life that have brought you a measure of joy. Then write "Great Joy!" beside Luke 2.*

SATURDAY, DECEMBER 23

"Blessed is she who has believed that the Lord would fulfill his promises to her!" Luke 1:45 (NIV)

As A CHILD I PICTURED Jesus' mother as sweet, gentle, caring—nearly perfect. Out of all the women in the world God picked her, right? She had to be someone special. As I've spent more time in God's Word I've discovered she's special for one reason most of all: Mary believed. In a song from her heart, Mary says:

"My soul glorifies the Lord
and my spirit rejoices in God my Savior,
for he has been mindful
of the humble state of his servant.
From now on all generations will call me blessed,
for the Mighty One has done great things for me—
holy is his name."
Luke 1:46–49 (NIV)

Mary's belief was where it should have been: on God. She accepted her role. She thanked God for her mission. And because of her belief generations of people have called her blessed and have thought of her as someone special.

This makes me wonder what things my disbelief causes me to miss out on. Only one woman was chosen to be Jesus' mother, but God has great missions designed for each of us. We simply need to realize He loves us most of all, His plans are perfect, and we can be part of those plans if we focus not on what we're lacking but rather on what He's offering. —TRICIA GOYER

FAITH STEP: *Have faith today to embrace Jesus' call and His special plan for you. What has Jesus asked you to do for Him? Are you willing to do it? To be called by God means He sees you as special.*

SATURDAY, DECEMBER 23

Jude, a servant of Jesus Christ and brother of James, to those who are called, beloved in God the Father and kept for Jesus Christ: May mercy, peace, and love be multiplied to you. Jude 1:1–2 (ESV)

MY SON AND HIS WIFE were expecting their third child close to Christmas. Big sister and brother seemed excited about the coming baby but a little uneasy about the change the birth would bring. Our five-year-old granddaughter asked her parents if they would love her less once the new baby arrived.

As we gathered around the Advent wreath in the living room, our son helped his daughter with an object lesson. He lit the first candle. "Your mommy and I love each other. This flame is like that love. Then we had you." He lit the second candle. "That didn't take away the light from the first candle, it added more. Then we had your brother." He lit another candle. "Did that take away any love from you? Of course not. Love keeps growing. Now when the new baby comes, we'll all have love for her too, but it will never take away the love we have for you."

My heart swelled as I listened, and memories swirled of my own wedding day, each of our children's births, and now our grandchildren's lives. Yet her question wasn't a silly one. Love is difficult. In our own power, we sometimes do feel depleted, unable to love each person Jesus brings across our path. Our own desires get in the way, our limitations exhaust us, and we need supernatural wisdom to figure out the best way to offer love to each unique person. Only our holy Savior is able to give us unselfish, unfailing, and perceptive relationships with family, friends, and even enemies. As we follow Jesus, He truly multiplies our love. —SHARON HINCK

FAITH STEP: *Light a candle. Ask Jesus to kindle His love in your heart, so that you can share it with others and watch it grow.*

SATURDAY, DECEMBER 23

I no longer call you servants, because a servant does not know his master's business. Instead, I have called you friends, for everything that I learned from my Father I have made known to you. John 15:15 (NIV)

I RECENTLY READ A SMALL book about the Swedish word *hygge* (pronounced hoo-gah), which means "cozy." Christmas traditions are hygge. Warm blankets and crackling fires are hygge. Flickering beeswax candles are hygge. But the most hygge thing of all is spending time with a close friend. I share a hygge relationship, built over decades of shared joy and struggles, with my cousin Beth. We understand each other. We pray for each other. We give each other a great amount of grace in the face of our weaknesses. We stand up for each other. After years of being in each other's lives, our hearts are knit together. I can go to Beth at any time and find empathy, hope, and some belly laughs. She gets me. She loves me. And she knows that she will receive the same love from me.

Close friendship is what we are created for. When Jesus came to this world, He didn't just come to bring salvation. He came to show us what real friendship is, laying down His very life for us. He came to engage us, laugh with us, and heal us. He delights in creating a path of joy for us. He gives us unimaginable grace and offers us refuge in His love. He intertwines His heart with ours, inviting us into an intimate relationship with Him. He gets us. He loves us. He calls us friends. He restores our souls. That is more than hygge (cozy). That is life-giving. —SUSANNA FOTH AUGHTMON

FAITH STEP: *Spend time with a close friend. Enjoy the fun you have in each other's presence. Thank Jesus for your friend and the gift of friendship that He offers you.*

LOVE

But let all who take refuge in you be glad;
let them ever sing for joy.
Spread your protection over them,
that those who love your name
may rejoice in you.

Psalm 5:11 (NIV)

SUNDAY, DECEMBER 24

But let all who take refuge in you rejoice; let them sing joyful praises forever. Spread your protection over them, that all who love your name may be filled with joy. Psalm 5:11 (NLT)

ONE OF MY FAVORITE CHRISTMAS MEMORIES happened when my kids were elementary-school age. We lived in Lacey, Washington, about eight hundred miles from my parents' home in Brooks, Alberta, Canada.

Driving to Brooks took nearly thirteen hours in the summer. That time increased dramatically in the winter. Consequently, my folks never expected us to visit for Christmas.

One year, we decided to make the journey but kept our plans a secret. We arrived at lunchtime on Christmas Eve and parked in the back alley, out of sight. Then we sent our kids to ring the doorbell. "Surprise!" the kids shouted when my mother opened the door.

"What on earth?" she exclaimed, then burst into happy tears.

If our appearance impacted them to that degree, imagine how the shepherds felt when a host of angels showed up as told in Luke 2:10–11 (NLT): "I bring you good news that will bring great joy to all people! The Savior—yes, the Messiah, the Lord—has been born today in Bethlehem, the city of David!"

Initial terror turned to wonder and delight when the shepherds saw the Savior incarnate, and they spread the good news to everyone they met before returning to their flocks, singing praise to God as they went.

This season we celebrate Jesus's coming to earth. Imagine: because of His arrival, we can experience joy—not just for one night or a season but for eternity. —GRACE FOX

FAITH STEP: *Luke 2:19 says that Mary pondered the events surrounding Jesus's birth in her heart. Pause today to ponder how His birth impacts your life and give Him thanks.*

SUNDAY, DECEMBER 24

"Come to me, all you that are weary and are carrying heavy burdens, and I will give you rest. Take my yoke upon you, and learn from me; for I am gentle and humble in heart, and you will find rest for your souls. For my yoke is easy, and my burden is light." Matthew 11:28–30 (NRSV)

IN THE CHRISTMAS CAROL "IT Came Upon a Midnight Clear," there is a little-known verse that contains this phrase: "Oh, hush the noise, ye men of strife, and hear the angels." The idea is that there is so much noise in our lives, and especially at Christmastime, that we may miss the message the angels brought to the shepherds and to us down through the ages—the good news for all people, that Jesus is born.

I like to sing this verse on the last Sunday of Advent, when Christmas festivities seem to ramp up at their most frenetic pace. It's a great reminder, and a great admonition. Noise doesn't hush on its own. We have to be deliberate about hushing it. Will we be carried away by the rolling tide of a modern consumer Christmas? Once again, our source of strength is silence and trust in Jesus.

The invitation always stands: *Come to Me. Rest.*

In Him we find the power to hush the noise. The wisdom to discern when and how and even whom to hush that the angels' message can be heard in our hearts: Peace…Goodwill…A Savior is born. —GWEN FORD FAULKENBERRY

FAITH STEP: *Take a few moments to "hush the noise" in your life today, and listen to the voice of Jesus inviting you into His rest.*

Sunday, December 24

But the angel said to them, "Do not be afraid. I bring you good news that will cause great joy for all the people. Today in the town of David a Savior has been born to you; he is the Messiah, the Lord . . . When they had seen him, they spread the word concerning what had been told them about this child, and all who heard it were amazed at what the shepherds said to them. Luke 2:10–11; 17–18 (NIV)

Our first grandchild was born on Christmas Eve. As soon as we received the call from our son-in-law, we headed out and drove several hours, eager to arrive in time for the birth.

The hospital looked deserted as the small crew of excited relatives waited in the halls outside our daughter's room. Not long after, we heard the loud cries of an infant. Our granddaughter was here! One glimpse of that baby girl filled everyone's hearts in that hospital room, from parents to each doting grandparent.

Smiles as big as Christmas, accompanied by tears of joy and baby brag books emerged from their hiding places. Those happy feelings didn't vanish the moment we left the hospital. No, we repeated those "sounding joys," as the familiar Christmas carol goes, to everyone who'd listen—each time a new grandchild was born. A new baby! Light of our lives! We would never be the same.

Over two thousand years ago a baby was born: the Son of God—Jesus, the long-awaited Savior. Just like us, the shepherds, on that starry night Jesus was born, couldn't keep the joy to themselves. Like us, they had to spread the good news of great joy to all who would listen. And because of Jesus, our lives—and theirs—changed forever. —Rebecca Barlow Jordan

Faith Step: *Read through or sing the words to the Christmas carol "Joy to the World." Then ask Jesus to help you "repeat the sounding joy" to someone who needs to hear that good news this Christmas.*

MONDAY, DECEMBER 25

Every good and perfect gift is from above, coming down from the Father of the heavenly lights, who does not change like shifting shadows. James 1:17 (NIV)

CHRISTMAS MORNING AT OUR HOUSE is a time of kids in pajamas with bedhead, gobbling breakfast and then listening to the Christmas story before opening presents. The celebration of Christ's birth is a time of excitement. It has also become a time of transformation for our family. Six years ago at Christmas we'd just met a birth mom who was considering our family for her soon-to-be born baby girl. (She chose us!) Three years ago this Christmas we were waiting for a call from DHS (Department of Human Services) and praying for the child(ren) Jesus had for us. A few weeks later we were matched with two siblings. Last year at Christmas we were praying about four sibling girls. This Christmas we have a FULL HOUSE with seven adopted children around the tree!

Not everyone's family grows exponentially like ours, but everyone can look to Christmas as a time to consider what we can offer: a welcoming hug, an understanding heart, even a place to belong.

God gave us His Son, Jesus. For my husband and me, His Son changed our hearts and opened our eyes to the needs of orphans. Those former orphans are transforming our Christmases. There is more noise around our house but also more life. The pile of presents is bigger, and the joy over every little gift is bigger too.

Jesus truly is the gift Who keeps on giving. As we follow Him, He teaches us to give, love, serve, embrace, and welcome. Just like He did. —TRICIA GOYER

FAITH STEP: *Thank Jesus for all the people—the perfect gifts—He's given to you. Say a prayer for each one as a special Christmas gift. Or write down your prayer and present it to everyone in your life on Christmas Day.*

MONDAY, DECEMBER 25

"But as for me, I will enter Your house through the abundance of Your steadfast love and mercy; I will worship . . . in reverent fear and awe of You." Psalm 5:7 (AMP)

I LOVE THAT VERSE. AND I think the reason I love it so much is that I often come to the Lord empty. Empty-handed, like a beggar clad in filthy rags, and also empty down in my soul, with a painful longing to be satisfied, and yet the knowledge that I have absolutely nothing to offer in the exchange. There's not a single, solitary reason He would want to let me enter His house. And yet. The Bible says I can enter through the abundance of His steadfast love and mercy.

I picture myself, this grubby pauper lifting a stained hand to knock on the door. But even before I can knock, the door is thrown open wide and my Father steps forward to greet me.

This relationship is a great mystery: how we can be loved with the familiarity of a family, totally secure knowing He is always with us and yet loved by a holy being who's so very different from us. *His ways are past finding out. He is high and lifted up.* He is totally different—beyond our comprehension. Bono, the lead singer of U2, said: "The idea that there's a force of love and logic behind the universe is overwhelming to start with.... But the idea that that same love and logic would choose to describe itself as a baby born in... straw and poverty is genius, and brings me to my knees, literally.... I am just in awe of that.... It's the thing that makes me a believer."

When I come to the Lord, one thing He gives me in exchange for my emptiness is awe. An awe that someone like Him would come to earth in order to save someone like me. What a mystery. What a Savior! —GWEN FORD FAULKENBERRY

FAITH STEP: *Embrace the mystery and the miracle of Your Savior today. Remember You are a pauper no more—but a child of the King.*

MONDAY, DECEMBER 25

For I am convinced that neither death nor life, neither angels nor demons, neither the present nor the future, nor any powers, neither height nor depth, nor anything else in all creation, will be able to separate us from the love of God that is in Christ Jesus our Lord. Romans 8:38–39 (NIV)

ABOUT SIXTEEN YEARS AGO, A woman experiencing homelessness walked into the emergency room of an Atlanta hospital in labor. Shortly after, she delivered a baby girl. She said she wanted the child to have a better life than what she could provide, and she specified that she wanted the baby to be raised in a Christian home. A social worker from the Christian foster agency Agape met with her in the hospital and learned of her wishes. She held the baby before she gave her to the social worker, named her little girl Ashley and told the baby that she wanted her to have a good life, a life in the Lord.

That precious baby was born with a mother's hope that she'd be raised loving her Lord and Savior. And then God blessed our family by putting that sweet baby in our home when she was merely two days old.

When I think about Ashley's mom showing up at that hospital in labor, I think about Mary arriving at the inn in Bethlehem. She and Joseph, like Ashley's mother, wanted their child to be loved. Christ's Heavenly Father also wants His child to be loved.

Today, on Christmas, remember the birth of our Savior. Remember how precious it is to raise a child to grow up loving Him, knowing Him, adoring Him. Even though Ashley's mother couldn't take care of her child physically, she took care of her spiritually by placing her in a Christian home. She knew how important it was for her little girl to know her Lord. —RENEE ANDREWS

FAITH STEP: *Today, while the world celebrates the birth of our Savior, take a moment to explain the miracle of Christ's birth to a child. Merry Christmas!*

The Birth of Jesus

In those days Caesar Augustus issued a decree that a census should be taken of the entire Roman world. (This was the first census that took place while Quirinius was governor of Syria.) And everyone went to their own town to register.

So Joseph also went up from the town of Nazareth in Galilee to Judea, to Bethlehem the town of David, because he belonged to the house and line of David. He went there to register with Mary, who was pledged to be married to him and was expecting a child. While they were there, the time came for the baby to be born, and she gave birth to her firstborn, a son. She wrapped him in cloths and placed him in a manger, because there was no guest room available for them.

And there were shepherds living out in the fields nearby, keeping watch over their flocks at night. An angel of the Lord appeared to them, and the glory of the Lord shone around them, and they were terrified. But the angel said to them, "Do not be afraid. I bring you good news that will cause great joy for all the people. Today in the town of David a Savior has been born to you; he is the Messiah, the Lord. This will be a sign to you: You will find a baby wrapped in cloths and lying in a manger."

Suddenly a great company of the heavenly host appeared with the angel, praising God and saying,

"Glory to God in the highest heaven,
and on earth peace to those on whom his favor rests."

When the angels had left them and gone into heaven, the shepherds said to one another, "Let's go to Bethlehem and see this thing that has happened, which the Lord has told us about."

So they hurried off and found Mary and Joseph, and the baby, who was lying in the manger. When they had seen him, they spread the word concerning what had been told them about this child, and all who heard it were amazed at what the shepherds said to them. But Mary treasured up all these things and pondered them in her heart. The shepherds returned, glorifying and praising God for all the things they had heard and seen, which were just as they had been told. —Luke 2:1–20 (NIV)

Advent and Christmas 2023
Reflections and Memories

Advent and Christmas 2023
Reflections and Memories

Advent and Christmas 2023
Reflections and Memories

Advent and Christmas 2023
Reflections and Memories

Advent and Christmas 2023
Reflections and Memories

Advent and Christmas 2023
Reflections and Memories

Advent and Christmas 2023
Reflections and Memories

Author Index

A Note from the Editors

We hope you enjoyed *Walking with Jesus: Devotions for Advent and Christmas,* published by Guideposts. For over 75 years, Guideposts, a nonprofit organization, has been driven by a vision of a world filled with hope. We aspire to be the voice of a trusted friend, a friend who makes you feel more hopeful and connected.

By making a purchase from Guideposts, you join our community in touching millions of lives, inspiring them to believe that all things are possible through faith, hope, and prayer. Your continued support allows us to provide uplifting resources to those in need. Whether through our communities, websites, apps, or publications, we inspire our audiences, bring them together, and comfort, uplift, entertain, and guide them. Visit us at guideposts.org to learn more.

We would love to hear from you. Write us at Guideposts, P.O. Box 5815, Harlan, Iowa 51593 or call us at (800) 932-2145. Did you love *Walking with Jesus?* Leave a review for this product on guideposts.org/shop. Your feedback helps others in our community find relevant products.

Find inspiration, find faith, find Guideposts.

Shop our best sellers and favorites at
guideposts.org/shop
Or scan the QR code to go directly to our Shop